The
Hidden
City

THE
HIDDEN
CITY

A Story of Aberdeen
and its People

ROBERT SMITH

JOHN DONALD PUBLISHERS LTD
EDINBURGH

First published in 1999 by
Birlinn Ltd
West Newington House
10 Newington Road
Edinburgh
EH9 1QS

www.birlinn.co.uk

Reprinted 2004

ISBN 0 85976 514 8

British Library Cataloguing-in-Publication Data
A catalogue record for this book is available
from the British Library

Typesetting and origination by Brinnoven, Livingston
Printed and bound in Great Britain by Antony Rowe Ltd, Chippenham

Preface

This is the story of two Aberdeens – one that we know and one that no longer exists. Many years ago the city was contained within what was known as the Royalty, an area defined by Royal charter. As the town spread out from the old boundaries it left behind a community 'crowded with buildings and abominably filthy', ravaged by disease and poverty – a city hidden behind the shining new thoroughfares that were part of the new Aberdeen. It was said that grandeur and meanness went side by side. This 'hidden city', with its rabbit-warren of courts and closes, is at the heart of this book. It recalls the time when Aberdeen was also a nameless city, and from there it moves out to look at how the city of today has developed – and how it faces the new Millenium.

In Part Two a picture is drawn of another 'hidden city'. The author, who was editor of the *Evening Express* for twenty-two years, describes how the newspaper industry was established in Aberdeen. He takes you behind the headlines to give you a glimpse of a newspaper at work. He recalls a column that was said to be 'the scourge of bureaucratic ineptitude'. He tells how newspapers over the years have crossed swords with the people who run the city, and of how the newspaper he himself edited had a strong and abiding link with its readers.

The book complements the author's highly succesful work, *The Granite City,* which was described by one reviewer as 'a delightfully told, wide-ranging kaleidoscope of city life'.

Contents

Part I
An Abominable City

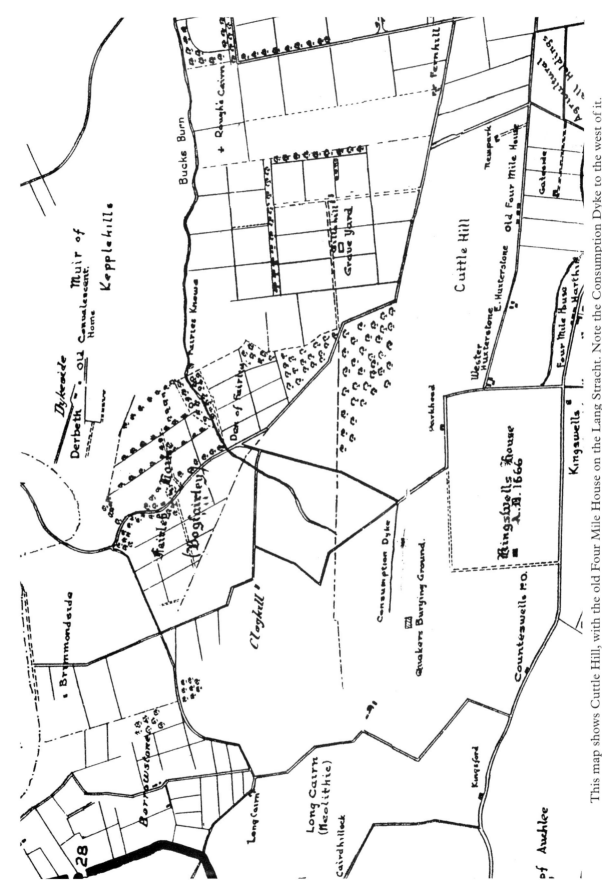

This map shows Cuttle Hill, with the old Four Mile House on the Lang Stracht. Note the Consumption Dyke to the west of it.

The Lang Stracht

Where the Lang Stracht shakes itself free of the city, pushing on to Kingswells by the old Skene road, it crosses an area of high ground shown on maps as the Cuttle Hill. This small hill on the outskirts of Aberdeen stands at the centre of the Stocket Forest, whose vast Freedom Lands were granted to Aberdeen by King Robert the Bruce in 1319 in recognition of the city's loyalty during the Wars of Independence.

Seventy years ago, Lord Provost James R. Rust drew the attention of his fellow citizens to the Cuttle Hill when he paid tribute to 'a great and upright Monarch' on the 600th aniversary of Bruce's death. He told them that the Cuttle Hill was the best place from which to survey the Freedom Lands, a viewpoint that would drive home the transformation that had been wrought by 'the town's tacksmen and vassals' in the course of six centuries.

The Town Council produced a commemorative book, *The Freedom Lands and Marches of Aberdeen*, with a preface signed by Lord Provost Rust and George S. Fraser, the town clerk. The book underlined the changes that had taken place in those six hundred years. It told how the hardy burghers of 1319 had seen 'a dreary waste, broken here and there by little thickets of trees and stunted brushwood, a wilderness of marshy bog and stony crag, a rude, primaeval, undeveloped heath', while their descendants in the early 20th century looked out on 'smiling, prosperous countryside, with orderly well cultivated fields producing luxuriant crops, interspersed with beautiful plantations'.

I went up Cuttle Hill to survey the Freedom Lands. Across the years the town had devoured more of that 'smiling countryside', creeping out towards Kingswells. Beyond the farmlands and the fields where Cocker's roses bloomed, the houses at Mastrick – 'cooncil hooses' – closed like a pincers on the Lang Stracht. In the distance the spires and rooftops of the city stretched away to the sea, where bulky oil supply boats waiting to enter the harbour languished like monstrous whales. It must have been on the edge of this oil-boom city, perhaps near Cuttle Hill, that G.S. Fraser, son of the town clerk who signed the Freedom book, found inspiration for his poem, *Hometown Elegy*.

In it he remembered 'the moorland paths and the country lying quiet and full of farms' on the outskirts of the town. It was from there that he looked across Aberdeen to the 'dying sprawl of the Dee' and saw the 'gas works, white ballroom, and the red brick baths, and salmon nets along a mile of shore'. The gas works and the red brick baths have gone, but the white ballroom is still there, while along the front the delights of pizza parlours, pool halls and popcorn are offered to the citizens of the new Millenium.

If Fraser had been standing there today, he would have marvelled at the vast spread of the city, and, perhaps, as I did, wondered at how all this had grown from a huddle of houses clustered around another hill, St Katherine's Hill. I thought of what the Lord Provost had told his fellow citizens in 1929. Forget for a moment the things of the present, he had urged, and glance backward across the centuries. He believed that the pages of the city's history carried lessons, not only for the present, but for the future, for succeeding generations.

Cuttle Hill (its name comes from the movement of corn from low ground to high ground for winnowing) was where the Aberdeen artist William Dyce was born in 1806. Today, it is virtually unknown. Eric MacIntosh, a teacher who lives in Gillahill Croft and knows the area well, had never heard of it, but Davie Simpson, at nearby Fernhill, knew about it.

It was only later that I found it marked on a map, 'Plan of the Freedom Lands of Aberdeen 1929', issued with the commemorative book. It is, in fact, the ground that borders the Lang Stracht near Newpark, where a track runs up to Gillahill and Fernhill. The hill rises gently, taking in the Lang Stracht, and drops down to Kingswells. The map shows the Old Four Mile House, on the south side of the hill, where travellers stopped for a glass of ale. Now they sip gin and tonics at a modern Four Mile House nearer the New Skene road.

When I was with Eric at Gillahill Croft, dusk was coming down on the city. Pinpoints of light were piercing the darkness like distant fireflies. It was impressive, but in daylight I found that there was no longer the unimpeded view that Lord Provost Rust had enjoyed. A reservoir had been built near Davie Simpson's farm and it had changed the whole outlook. Gillahill Farm lies at the end of a track leading to the Bucks Burn and the Muir of Kepplehills.

The name Gillahill is said to mean a cattle fold, but another theory is that it is a distortion of Gallow Hill, where hangings took place. At anyrate, it is no place to be on a dark night, for there are worse things than the hangman's rope. On the farm is a graveyard where resurrectionists are said to have buried their dismembered corpses. It seems an unlikely story, although there could be no better place to bury bodies if the law was on your tail.

Graham Gauld, who farms Gillahill, took me to his door and pointed to a small woodland across the fields. 'That's where the graveyard is supposed to be', he said, 'but you won't find any graves there'. He had never heard the body-snatching tale. He had been told it was a Quakers' graveyard, and, in fact, some American Quakers had once come to see it. From time to time, students knock on his door and ask about it. It is possible, however, that this 'graveyard' has been confused with a Quakers' burying ground shown farther west on the Freedom Lands map.

I followed a narrow footpath into the wood and found nothing that hinted at burials or body-snatchers. Through the trees I could see a new housing estate that had been built on the edge of it. Kingswells seems to spread its octupus arms all around the area, which is why it is not as 'full of farms' as it was in G.S. Fraser's day. But away from the new roads and smart new houses old farms still cling to the uncompromising land. Here, so near the city, there is a sense of almost total isolation. The farm roads are stony and overgrown. Great pot-holes shake your bones as you drive slowly over them. Long stalks of wild rose-bay willow herbs line the roadside, their cerise heads nodding in the breeze.

The 1929 Freedom book has a photograph taken in the Quakers' wood, looking across the fields to Gillahill Farm and a tall chimney-stack that rises above the farm buildings. This huge red-brick chimney seems to underline the fact that Gillahill has one foot in the past, as do other farms that lie, or lay, on the fringes of Brimmond Hill – Bogfairley, Moss-side, Overhill, Redmyres. They hint at an endless struggle against the 'primeval heath' of Bruce's time. There is a farm called Hope, which makes you wonder what tremulous fears gave rise to such a name. William Forsyth, the Aberdeen poet, summed it up in this verse:

> An' then-o'-days the countryside
> To Brimmond an' the Loch o' Skene,
> Wis ae bleak muir, o' sax miles wide,
> Wi' scarce a single patch o' green.

When reiving caterans came raging down from the hills in search of plunder, they found 'scarcely a cow to steal'. It was in this stony wasteland north of the Bucks Burn that a farm called Dykeside was built. Dykeside – 'full of stones', it was said – was known to Francis Douglas, an Aberdeen baker, bookseller and newspaper owner, who wrote *A General Description of the East Coast of Scotland* in 1780. He drew attention to the rapid changes that had taken place in Aberdeen, particularly in the common pastureland. 'In the bottom are many bleachfields made out from swamps and morasses', he wrote, and he noted that the 'under-part' of the Stocket had been feued out by the town.

But a different scene faced him when he climbed 'the eminence called the Stocket-brae. 'When we reached the summit of this little hill', he wrote, 'an extensive, but wild prospect opened up to the west and south-west, in which little was to be seen but heath and moor. We rode two miles further west to see a farm called Dykeside. Much of the ground was full of great stones, which obstructed the plough. To consume them, after they were blown and cut, some of the fences were built five feet thick at the bottom'.

To *consume* them, said Douglas, as if some monolithic creature had come out of the thickets and swallowed them up. What did swallow them up were Douglas's so-called 'fences' – Consumption Dykes. A number were built in Newhills parish long after Douglas's book was published. For a time, some could be seen by the side of the Lang Stracht, but they were pulled down in 1934 and used for road-making. William Adam, a Bucksburn man who owned Hope Farm, made double dykes. These were set apart from each other so that trees could be planted between them.

A Shetland writer, Catherine Sinclair, visiting Aberdeen in 1840, saw the stony land near the city and wrote: 'You might fancy, in some parts of this country, that it rained stones instead of water!' She described how she saw a 6ft-high dyke which was 'twenty or thirty feet' broad, fit for a wagon to be driven on and looking as if materials had been collected for erecting a village'. This was the West Dyke, which was approximately 500 yards long and 27 feet wide and ran from west to east in four sections across four fields 440 yards north of the Mains of Kingswells.

The West Dyke was constructed by Dr Francis Edmond, who bought the Kingswells estate in 1854. He was said to have built the dyke, not only to clear the stones, but so that he could have a dry elevated walk over his property. The East Dyke continued eastwards in 'a nicely-shaped walk through a plantation to the limit of Kingswells estate on Goose Hill'.

In 1876, another woman visitor to Kingswells saw 'fields strewn with boulders, shattered fragments of great rocks'. Some of the dykes, she said, reminded her of Babylon's great walls. She also wrote about stones being built 'into a monster mound'. This 'monster mound' was said to lie west of the reservoir, near Gillahill Farm. A number of these consumption dykes can still be seen at Kingswells, including one which starts at Kingswood Avenue and runs between the main road and a public park. There is a break in the dyke where the stones have been put together as steps, so that people with steady legs can walk along the top of the dyke.

But I was looking for Babylon's great walls . . . and the 'monster mound'. Davie Simpson told me how to get there from Fernhill Farm. His instructions were explicit. I had to follow the track past the reservoir. Beyond the farmhouse there was a sequence of fields . . . a grass field, a barley field, a grass field, a barley field, and another grass field. At this last grass field – the fifth field – I would see Rough's Cairn. Rough's Cairn, marked on the map, was named after the farmer on whose land it stood, and I had a suspicion that this was the 'monster mound'.

Davie said it was about a mile away and warned me that I would have to climb a few dykes. He didn't mention the barbed wire. But down the road I

The Consumption Dyke at Kingswells, running between the main road and a public park.

went, yellowing fields of barley on my left, cattle bellowing dolefully on my right, on over two gates to a track bordering the fifth field. At the end of it I found myself surrounded by consumption dykes, 'Babylon's great walls', and in the distance I could see Rough's Cairn. The field I had to cross to reach it was wet and muddy. Heavy rain had fallen. I squelched through the sodden grass, understanding now why the consumption dykes had been a boon to Dr Francis Edmond, who enjoyed 'a dry elevated walk over his property'.

I climbed on to one of the dykes to get a better view of Rough's Cairn. Here, as the Shetland writer Catherine Sinclair had said, it looked as if it had rained stones as well as water. Huge boulders had been piled on top of each other to form a massive cairn, and at the foot of it a line of stones stretched away in a

'Babylon's great walls' – the Consumption Dyke near the new housing estate at Kingswells.

long tail. There was a photograph of the cairn in the Freedom book, looking in distant silhouette like some stony-tailed monster. The caption to the picture gave its measurements: 300ft long, 20ft broad, and 20ft high. It was built about 1850, twenty-six years before the visit of the woman who had written about these 'monster mounds'.

Here, progress had finally caught up with the consumption dykes. Ignored and forgotten for so many years, they were now not much more than a stone's throw from the expanding town, sitting in the shadow of a big new housing scheme. If Dr Francis Edmond had been alive he would probably have attempted to stop this house-building mania, for he once created a great stir by erecting a cottage across the old Skene road to stop its use on his estate.

Behind the houses and the dykes a wide patch of brown moorland could be seen, a tiny corner of William Forsyth's poetic landscape – 'ae brown muir o' sax miles wide'. In the distance was Brimmond Hill, with its straggling line of masts. But I was going in the opposite direction, back to another hill, Cuttle Hill, to take a last look across the Freedom Lands.

Below me on Cuttle Hill bulldozers were hacking a new road out of the Lang Stracht, a road built to cater for the daily torrent of traffic from Kingswells and Westhill. It meant that a small section of the old road would be consigned to history. The Freedom map showed two farms on this section, Wester Huxterstone and Easter Huxterstone, whose names were a reminder of the huxters or hawkers of an earlier age. Those names, like Broadykes and Edmond Gardens, are now Kingswells street names.

George M. Fraser, writing about the old Skene Road in the *Aberdeen Free Press* in 1918, said that it was 'a fine old road, well used, and for the most part well kept throughout its course'. Today, sections of it are still in use on the approaches to Westhill. The farm of Brodiach, near Westhills, was once a hostelry – the Six-Mile House – and other farms like Gateside (the 'gait' or way along the Lang Stracht) recalled bygone days.

Looking east from Cuttle Hill, the Lang Stracht slips into the town beyond a side-road linking it with the main route from Hazlehead to Westhill and Raemoir. Maidencraig Mill was originally regarded as the end of the Lang Stracht. G.M. Fraser gave its length as 'a mile and three-quarters in a straight line, till you pass Maidencraig'. Its starting point was the Cocket Hat, which took its name from a small triangular field on the property of Raeden, owned by George More, twice Provost of the town in the late 18th and early 19th centuries. Most people, however, think of the Cocket Hat as a hotel that stood there for many years. It was finally demolished to make way for a new hotel, with an *English* cocket hat on its roof.

I came down from Cuttle Hill and made my way back into town by the Lang Stracht, not the old dusty road, but a bright, wide, dual carriageway. G.M. Fraser once said that in walking citywards along the Lang Stracht you were walking through the history of Aberdeen. I was thinking this as I tramped along it . . . and thinking, too, of the call made by Lord Provost James Rust all those years ago. Glance back across the centuries, he had said, for the pages of the city's history carried lessons for the future. In the last year of the 20th century it was a message that still held good. The Lang Stracht – old and new – was a good place to start.

CHAPTER ONE

The Stocket Head

A map of Aberdeen drawn up by Parson James Gordon of Rothiemay in 1661 shows houses climbing up the Gallowgate to a 'Wynde Mill' at the top of the brae. Nudging a long row of buildings and gardens on this historic street is 'The Marrisch Called the Loch' – the Loch of Aberdeen – and beyond the loch a faint track can be seen running west from Gallowgate Hill. This is marked on the map as the 'Way to the Stoked Heade'.

For most of my life I have lived in the shadow of the Stocket 'way'. I was born in a tenement house on the edge of it, went to school there, delivered morning 'rowies' and evening papers to its householders, tramped up its long brae as a boy, and looked down on the city from the 'Stoked Heade' when the street gas lamps were lit by leeries. Until recently, I still had a home within sight of it.

Today, there is only one Stocket road to commemorate King Robert the Bruce's gift of the Freedom Lands to the city – Mid Stocket Road, sometimes called the North Stocket Road. Originally there were three, including the Low Stocket Road, which became Westburn Road, and the South Stocket Road, which ran from Mile End and became Beechgrove Terrace and King's Gate.

In Parson Gordon's time, the whole length of the old highway from the Gallowgate to Kingswells was known as the Stocket Road. In September, 1665, four years after he had drawn up his map, the town council granted a piece of waste ground near the Loch of Aberdeen to a Walter Melville, who had reclaimed part of the loch and wanted to build a house and barn at the west end of it – 'neir to the commone hieway going from the toune to the Burk Mill, near the lands of Dub Castell'. As the town developed, new names were given to sections of this 'commone hieway', among them Spring Garden and Maberley Street, linking the Gallowgate to the high ground of Gilcomston and Rosemount.

Nearly two centuries after Melville's approach to the council, William Forsyth, the Aberdeen poet, wrote a poem describing how the Loch of Aberdeen – 'the misty loch' – had once been 'white wi' geese'. Now, he went on, 'the geese are dead, and where they fed five hunder weel-fill't hooses stan'.

By the end of the 19th century many more 'weel-fill't hooses' had been built. In 1829 the first street to carry the district name, Rosemount Terrace, was laid

The tenement house in Wallfield Place where the author was born.

out, and in 1847 another development, Mount Street, was announced – 'A New Street having been formed through the Lands of Rosemount, leading from the Old Skene Road towards the Mid Stocket Road, opposite the Lunatic Asylum, building areas will now be feued along the street'. Prospective house-buyers were told that Mount Street was 'airy', with 'a delightful view of the surrounding country'.

The town continued to push westward up the old Stocket road. By January, 1860, it had extended to Mount Street on the south side of Rosemount and to Short Loanings on the north side. The demand for new housing was accelerated by the building of the Rosemount-Denburn Viaduct, a development almost as ambitious as the laying-out of Union Street. The city's population rose from 63,000 in 1841 to 135,00 in 1901, and at the turn of the century Rosemount stood on the threshold of a golden age of tenement building.

The lands of Rosemount, spreading across a ridge of high ground between the Den Burn and the West Burn, were dotted with country mansions. Some are still there today, now put to another use, while the names of others are perpetuated in the streets of houses that replaced them. Rosemount House, built before 1810, survives. This two-storey block, which gave its name to the district, is now hemmed in by tenements and reached by a pend on Rosemount Place.

North of the Low Stocket Road was the estate of Berryden, owned by an eccentric druggist called Alexander Leslie. He knew Alexander Jaffray of Kingswells and often went there to shoot crows. He thought they were nearly as good to eat as chickens. Jaffray, in his *Recollections of Kingswells,* recalled seeing him in Aberdeen in 1777 'near the city'. He had, said Jaffray, built a house and laid out a garden 'in a singular fashion of his own, with minute walks and childish grottos'.

Francis Douglas wrote about how he visited Sandy Leslie's villa at Berryden and was given a tour of the estate. The druggist took him through the grounds to 'an elegant bathing room, where by turning a cock you may raise the water to what depth you please, or let it run off at the other end'. He was then shown a grotto which had 'a cell devoted to serious contemplation'. One wall was divided up into little squares, each carrying 'some striking passage from an author of good repute'. In another small room he saw 'a small urn, with a label upon it, in memory of a lady who has been some years dead'.

The crow-eating druggist belonged to a part of Aberdeen that I knew well. Back in the fifties I lived in a tenement house in Chestnut Row, a dead-end street off Berryden Road. It was one of three short streets running parallel to each other, all named after trees, but there were only two scraggy trees in my street, and no chestnuts. The youngsters in the Row all went down to play in what they called 'the woodies'. Opposite 'the woodies' was an alley which gloried in the name of the Golden Lane. It led to Stewart's shoppie and to Elm Place and Cedar Place. A laundry (now turned into housing) stood at the top of Chestnut Row and over a high wall was the Royal Cornhill Hospital, shown in maps at the turn of the century as the Royal Lunatic Asylum.

There was no massive Norco Super-store in the field opposite Chestnut Row in those days. Alexander Leslie thought it a 'pretty little romantic place'. He took his morning walk there, breathing in 'the treasures of the atmosphere'. In 1953 the pretty little romantic place became the setting for a Coronation celebration organised by the Chestnut Row residents. They put up a marquee in the field, held a picnic and a fancy-dress parade, and set up tables in the street. Lord Provost John Graham came along and the Lady Provost formally opened the event. Each youngster was presented with a Bible. I wrote about

One of the ponds at the Westburn Park, where the author played as a boy.

the celebrations in the *Evening Express* and described Chestnut Row as 'the dead-end street with live ideas', a phrase that was thrown back at me long after the event.

Leslie died in 1799 at the age of seventy-seven. The grotto was cleared away in 1926 when Berryden House was demolished to make way for the 'Co-opy' dairy premises. A near neighbour of the eccentric druggist was a Mr Innes, a Commissary-Clerk, who lived in the mansion house of Clerkseat and was 'the richest man that ever held office'. He was 'the happy father of six sons and eleven most amiable daughters'. His house, however, was said to be overshadowed as a show place in 1780 by Leslie's villa. To the west of Clerkseat was Loch-head House, which became Scotland's first hydropathic. In 1873 it was used as a convalescent hospital by the Royal Infirmary and about twenty years later was bought by the town.

Westburn Park and its burn, which was sometimes called Clerkseat Burn or Gilcomston Burn, has misty memories for me. The burn was a magnet for youngsters when I was a boy, and still is today. Rising in Mastrick, it comes bouncing out of nowhere, splashing boisterously through paddling pools and under little stone bridges before disappearing into a black hole at the east end

Westburn House, designed by Archibald Simpson.

of the park. I remember how we dropped sticks into it and watched them race each other into the tunnel, wondering if they would ever see daylight again, and if so, where they would surface.

Up on the brae above the burn was Westburn House, a stately mansion that conjured up visions of horse-drawn carriages rattling up the park's long tree-lined avenue to the west door of the house, where elegant ladies stepped down to enter the mansion by a striking Greek portico. This entrance has been described as 'pure Simpson'. The house was designed by Archibald Simpson in 1836–39 and a later addition on the south side was a roofed veranda with slim wrought-iron columns and a low balustrade. The north side had three storeys and a sunken basement.

I once had a vested interest in that gloomy basement. The house was built for David Chalmers, printer and grandson of James Chalmers, founder of the *Aberdeen Journal,* whose firm was to shape my career more than a century later. The property, known as West Burn of Rubislaw, belonged to ex-Provost George More of Raeden in 1810. It was bought by the town council in 1901, but little imagination has been shown in the use of a building designed by Aberdeen's famous architect. Westburn House was turned into a tea room (tea and coffee served on the open veranda), but with refreshments now available in the nearby bowling pavilion it has virtually become redundant. When its glory days were over, it became *my* home for a time. There were no servants to usher me in by the west door. I had to enter by the back door – into a sunken basement.

This came about at the end of the war when, 'demobbed', married and hunting for a home, I discovered that the only way to get one was to pay 'key money' to the landlord. In the end I had to do this, but in the meantime a family friend came to the rescue. She was always known as 'Nanna' Kean, and this lovable lady ran the tearoom and a 'shoppie' in Westburn's big house. She gave us the use of the basement, which was reached by an entrance at the back of the house. There, down cold stone steps, was the room we had been given. It was dark and claustrophobic, but it was our first home.

Farther north on the Low Stocket Road was Woodhill House, which dated from the late 18th century. It was demolished in 1975 to make way for local authority offices, but the name Woodhill House was retained. Across the road was the site of Raeden House, a Georgian mansion partly built by an Aberdeen merchant, Gilbert More, and passed on to his son, Provost George More of Raeden. This highly distinctive building also became a victim of the bureaucratic axe, It was bought by Aberdeen city council and demolished in 1954. Raeden is now a council housing estate and a school stands on the site of the old mansion house. Before the streets were laid, the land east of Raeden was a moor – Bonnie Moor, which gave its name to Bonnymuir Place.

Bonnymuir, Woodhill, Stockethill, Cornhill, Foresterhill, Elmhill, Belvidere, Wallfield . . . old maps are peppered with the names of mansion houses swallowed up by the burgeoning city of last century. One vanished mansion had a special significance for me – Wallfield, or Well-field, near Belvidere House. An advertisement in the *Aberdeen Journal* of 1826 read: 'To let, the Property of Wallfield, formerly called Belvidere, on the Stocket Road'. The house was said to be capable of accommodating a large family and attached to it was 'a Well, Wash-house, Dry-house, and Laundry, and a Byre, with a garden of about half an acre, well stocked with fruit trees, berry bushes, flowers, etc'.

The name was perpetuated in two streets, Wallfield Place and Wallfield Crescent, and it was in a tenement in Wallfield Place that I was born. There were no poems in stone in the builder's mind when they built the granite tenements in Wallfield. Down in the lower reaches of Rosemount Viaduct there were tenements 'dressed in Sunday best . . . pretending to be a mansion block of flats such as were currently becoming the vogue in London',* but when you climbed up to the Stocket road the houses were plain and unadorned. The only 'mod cons' they had were a sink in the window, a bed recess, a wash-house in the 'backie', and gas lamps and toilets on the landings. The 'lavies' had toilet paper cut from the pages of the *Evening Express* and hung on a hook on the wall.

---

*W. A. Brogden's *Aberdeen, an Illustrated Architectural Guide*.

In those pre-war tenements in the Rosemount area you were living in a kind of no-man's land between working class and middle class. Those who looked down their noses at the working class locked their front doors and had keys for each of the six tenants. The Aberdeen poet Alistair Mackie certainly saw such tenements as working class homes – 'The nippit livin-rooms o the workin class afore the war', he wrote, 'the sink aye a sotter o pottit plants and the leavins o denner-time . . . the side-boord and table, the shewin machine . . . the sense o a human steer ye couldna redd up'.

When I wrote *The Granite City* I said that Aberdeen was a tenement town. That was ten years ago, when the book's first edition was published, and today it is truer than ever before. Tenement schemes – blocks of flats – have mushroomed all over the city. The 165-year-old John Knox Church on the city's Mounthooly roundabout was where my wife and I were married. In the summer of 1998 plans were drawn up to convert it into 35 *apartments*. There were also plans to knock down a warehouse on Sunnybank Road and build a three-and-a-half storey block of twenty-one flats. It seemed that whenever a spare piece of land was spotted the builders moved in.

Today, such properties are presented for sale in the polished phrases of the 'ad' man. They are no longer called tenements; 'flats' and 'apartments' are more socially acceptable. The dictionary definition of a tenement is 'a large building, usually of three or more storeys, divided into *flats* for separate householders', but one dictionary gives the definition as 'a large slum house divided into rooms or flats for let'. Davie Duncan, who wrote *Tenements and Sentiments*, would have agreed with the second definition, for he opened up the darker side of the tenement world in Aberdeen, part of the 'hidden city' written about in this book.

The solid, respectable tenements on Rosemount had little in common with the 'decaying primitive dwellings' he had known in Gilcomston, where he was born. He would wander up Skene Street, with its 'menial parade of tenements and dingy shops', and, going on to Whitehall Place and Esslemont Avenue, would see with a jaundiced eye the Grammar School, a 'symbol of patronage and entrenched privilege'. There, he said, 'they supped the cream of education, while we got skimmed milk and made the best of it'.

Davie, exploring the back-streets of Rosemount, would often hear the Broadford bell calling the mill workers to their daily toil. 'If anybody was late', he said, 'the gates were closed and a day's pay was forfeited; you had to pay for your sins'. That was true, but there was an old poem about Broadford that had bairnies louping for joy at the sight of its reeking lums, knowing that their da would get his wages every Thursday, that the 'bassies' (bowl) was full of meal again and that there were bannocks on the board.

That great red-brick Bastille of a building on the Stocket Road – it is actually called the Bastille – has always seemed to me to be one of the city's ugliest

The avenue through Westburn Park to Westburn House.

buildings, yet John R. Allan declared: 'Broadford is *not* offensive'. He thought that the very fact that it was brick in a granite town made it remarkable.. 'By some trick of association', he said, 'it has for a long time reminded me of Hampton Court'. It seemed a curious comparison, but Allan might have thought his case proven if he had lived to see the Broadford works today – turned into expensive luxury flats.

Stevenson Street also got a mention in *Tenements and Sentiments*. Laid out before the construction of the Viaduct, it ran parallel to Rosemount Viaduct, dropping down to the Denburn. According to Davie, it was 'a dark, mean street, with hallways like dark tunnels, rickety, well-worn lobbies, staircases and landings'. He added that the tenants had 'a liberal supply of cut-up *Evening Expresses* in the ochre-daubed boxes which served as WCs. Stevenson Street was considered as a possible direct route between Rosemount and the Denburn, but it too was overtaken by new developments.

I remember meeting Davie when I was editor of the *Evening Express*. He was a regular contributor to the newspaper's letter pages. I didn't know then that we had something in common; we had both been pupils of Rosemount School. I had gone there from Mile-End, while he had been at Skene Street, but our secondary schooling was separated by a number of years. Nevertheless, his *Tenements and Sentiments* jogged my memory. Reading it, I was seeing the faces of old 'Mount' teachers, among them George Dickie, the maths master, who was 'likeable and efficient' and had a highly accurate aim with pieces of chalk. There was Corker Ross, whose leg had been blown off in the first world war. Corker, who taught poetry appreciation, called his pupils 'fat, lazy lumps of human flesh'.

When I went back to Rosemount School to revive fading memories I drove down Belgrave Terrace, which branches off Esslemont Avenue amd flanks one side of the school. I looked through the iron railings and found to my astonishment that they were building flats in my old playground. Was there no end to it? I drove on, thinking of those half-forgotten school days, of bunsen burners flickering on the desks of the science room near the flats, of the vanished woodwork room, where I made a pipe rack for my father (he never used it), and of 'Fatty' Innes, the music teacher, winding up an old-fashioned gramophone and saying with a comical leer, 'Music by Handel!' He wasn't always so jocular. For a teacher who was trying to pour music into the souls of his pupils he had a strange leaning towards the 'scud'.

Cuthbert Graham, who was my editor on the old *Weekly Journal,* said in his *Historical Walk-about of Aberdeen,* that the school was 'a stately structure in the classical Italianate style'. Of course, he was right, but I always thought of it as a dour, plain building. Steps plunged down from Rosemount Place to the playground, but I was happiest climbing up them and into the bustling world above. Davie Duncan remembered it as 'a huge impressive building of granite with a big entrance door that led to a flight of stairs and a hall where we were all to assemble'. The school was designed by James Souttar and built in 1883-4. I have sometimes wondered what Davie would have said if he had known that it was to become for a time a satellite of the Grammar School. Now it is a community education centre.

The lofty tenements of Esslement Avenue, plunging down from Rosemount School to the Grammar School, that 'symbol of patronage and privilege', always seemed to me to be a kind of boundary line. I was on familiar territory, looking up to Mile End and the way to the Stocket Head. I remember the pre-war shops that never seemed to change . . . Sang's, the newsagent's; the 'chipper' in Wallfield Crescent; McWilliam's, the butcher; Thomson's sweetie shop, whose huge window was packed with confectionery; and Strathdee, the baker, whose rowies my brothers and I delivered. My elder brother, Ted, once left a tap on in the back shop and flooded the place. George Strathdee dubbed him 'the water engineer'.

I remember the lane that ran down from Rosemount to the Victoria Park, and the bakery stables that were half-way down the lane. We helped to look after the horses there, great clomping Clydesdales, and we smoked cinnamon sticks with an air of bravado. When we were older we graduated to puffing Woodbines at the back of Macpherson's garage on Craigie Loanings. I remember, too, the No. 5 tramcar rattling up from the Viaduct to Mile End and Beechgrove, where it broke away on its 'Circle' route to Queen's Cross. Alistair Mackie, the Aberdeen poet, living in Baker Street, could hear 'the gaitherin thunder o the trams as they shoogled back and fore fae the toun'. They shoogled past unassuming streets like Watson Street and Thomson Street, named after a shoemaker, Baillie George Watson and James Thomson, a valuator. Belvidere was a more sophisticated name. G. M. Fraser said it was 'fanciful'. I always wondered what particular mile was marked by Mile End, but it seemed that it was 'an importation'.

When you climb up the old Mid Stocket road and look out over the houses sprawling away to the west, it is hard to imagine that this was once the Stocket Forest, granted to Aberdonians in 1313 by Robert the Bruce. Wolves prowled through it, deer fed in it (four Keepers of the Forest were fined eight pennies in 1398 for destroying them), and robbers found shelter there.

The city magistrates, anxious to deprive marauders of their cover, allowed citizens to take wood from the forest to 'add balconies to the fronts of their houses, projecting eight or ten feet into the street'. Nowadays, they add conservatories to the backs of their houses. Maybe the balconies will make a comeback in the next century.

CHAPTER TWO
The Steps

A street sign, 'Gilcomston Steps', can be seen on a building near Aberdeen's Woolmanhill. People going up the Gilcomston brae must wonder where the steps are, or what happened to them, for there is nothing to justify the name or to indicate its origin. The street is no more then 100 yards long, which suggests that that there *was* a long flight of steps or stairs, not simply a street. On the other hand, G.M. Fraser, in his *Aberdeen Street Names*, warned his readers not to jump to the wrong conclusion. 'We are not to suppose', he wrote, 'that, although the street here forms a slight ascent, it was ever actually a stair like the streets of certain Continental towns'.

The street sign is at the corner of Raeburn Place. Farther up is the Gilcomston Bar, with a sign outside its door depicting 'Gillycoam's Toun' as it was back through the centuries. Beyond Baker Street are two shops and two large billboards. This is where Gilcomston Steps ends. Here, another street sign says 'Skene Square', with an arrow pointing up the hill. It is, as G.M. Fraser observed, all 'a little puzzling'.

There were steps in Gilcomston in the early 18th century, leading from high ground to what was known as Nether Gilcomston. These were seen in Paterson's Map of 1746, recorded simply as 'The Steps', but when the road became a public highway the name was changed to 'The Steps of Gilcomston'. In 1852 it took its present form, 'Gilcomston Steps'.

So the mystery of 'The Steps' and their link with the hamlet of Gilcomston remains unsolved. It isn't the only mystery. Here, in what was once one of the most ancient suburbs of Aberdeen, history has been turned on its head. This corner of Rosemount is an onomastics nightmare. Why, for instance, is the street leading up from Gilcomston Steps called Skene Square when there isn't a square in sight? G.M. Fraser said this question was 'really more difficult than the "Steps" themselves'. He came across an advertisement in the *Aberdeen Journal* in April, 1807, which offered 'extensive premises called Skene Square' for sale. The premises were used for 'cart and plough work'. Fraser thought that they probably stood on the site of Skene Square School. Just to complicate matters, the street was sometimes known as Skene's Square.

Then there is Gilcomston itself, generally thought to be a Celtic name meaning Gilcolm's-town. Back in 1853, a writer called Archibald Courage had other ideas. He wrote a book, *A Brief Survey of Aberdeen,* in which he said that

The sign above the Gilcomston Bar.

going up Skene Square from Woolmanhill you came upon a garden in which there was 'the stone from which this suburb has its name'. In other words, Gilcolm's-stone, not Gilcolm's-town. This theory was given some weight by the fact that Paterson's Map showed '2 stones of 6 and 12 feet high'.

Rotten Holes is another name that beats the experts. It was a name given to houses in Gilcomston in the middle of the 19th century – 'mean and pitiful

Gilcomston Steps. Note the windows level with the pavement.

hovels' whose red-brick walls were black with dirt. William Walker, author of *The Bards of Bon-Accord*, remembered seeing them as a youth. 'How the "biggin's" got the name of "Rotten Holes" I never knew', he said, 'but even then there was a smack of the old world about their sadly dilapidated aspect. The floor of each 'housie' was sunk considerably below the street level and was reached by steps from the outer door'. The last house had six steps going down to the kitchen.

In 1818 the population of Gilcomston was 'upwards of 1500'. It was now regarded as a suburb of Aberdeen. The commonty and barren wastes that lay around it had been cleared of stones, drained and trenched, enclosed 'at an immense expense' and converted into cornfields, villas and gardens. But its future was less than rosy. No plan had been made for future development and Gilcomston went into decline. By the 1850s it had become a village of tumbledown tenements. These old 'biggins' were swept away by the coming of the Denburn Valley railway in 1865-67 and by the building of Rosemount Viaduct.

The Gilcomston district covered the area between Skene Street and Rosemount Place on one side and Spa Street, Skene Square and Short Loanings on the other, but by the end of the 19th century it had been more or less merged in the expanding Rosemount district. It was a weaving community. Weavers sang at their looms, among them a poet called John Maclean, whose bitter verse cried out against 'fat lairds' who preached the gospel and starved

Housewives do their washing in the Denburn, with the new Union Bridge and the old Bow Brig in the background.

the poor. He had harsh words for the 'rich, big-bellied passers-by' who ignored the less well-off:

> Wi' granite hearts and cheeks as dry
>   As burning sun;
> They seldom think that soon they'll lie
>   Beneath the grun'.

Maclean, born at Gilcomston in 1795, lost his mother, was abandoned by his father, and wandered the countryside looking for work. When he complained to one employer about the 'abominable filth' on his bed he was warned that a better bed would be found for him in the Bridewell – the West Prison in Rose Street. Later, he worked in another 'filthy abode' in Aberdeen. The house and workshop were in 'a dark and narrow court named after the proprietor, Burr's Court, next to the old Castle Gallowgate'. Burr was his employer.

John turned a jaundiced eye on the human race in general. He wrote a poem about Johnny, a souter, who was 'wore out wi' shoemakin' and feasted on turnips like a hungry stirk rather than work. One of his poems was entitled 'Epitaph on a Blustering Fool' –

> Nae mair he'll guzzle doon the whisky,
> Nor fight wi' tykes when mad and frisky,

> Ah, Tam, gin' ye'r among the soot,
> Ye'll hae to fecht ere ye win oot.

Maclean's verses were dismissed as 'unconsidered trifles', but there were other poets, like William Sutherland, known as the 'Gilcomston poet', whose work was highly praised. Gilcomston and neighbouring Woolmanhill produced a remarkable number of poets and writers who made their mark in the world; it was said that there were more literary landmarks there than anywhere else in Aberdeen.

Nowadays, it is difficult to feel any real sense of the past when you go down the Gilcomston Steps and into Woolmanhill, an area that has changed out of all recognition in recent years. Below Skene Square a dual carriageway hurtles you towards the Denburn, and roundabouts pitch you out into streets whose names go far back into the city's history. Some names are unchanged, others have vanished, and a few have been altered; Shuttle Street, for instance, a weaver's street, which inexplicably became St Andrew's Street. Then there is Blackfriars Street, laid out in the monastery garden of the Chapel of the Black Friars; and Crooked Lane, which passes the back gate of Robert Gordon's Hospital, better known as Robert Gordon's College.

The founder of Robert Gordon's Hospital, who lived and died a bachelor, had one ambition – to be rich. Francis Douglas passed on a waspish piece of gossip about him. 'One would blush', he wrote, 'to repeat some stories told of his sordid economy'. He saved not only on food but on fuel, and he possessed, said Douglas, a happy secret – how to extract heat from coal without consuming it. He did this by putting a large hot coal into a basket with a rope fixed to it – and then carried it up and down the room till he felt warm enough.

Whatever his miserly tendencies, he was a great benefactor to the town and the magistrates gave him a princely burial. He was buried with military honours, with cannon placed at high points around the town. Bells rang out as the burial service took place and minute-guns were fired. 'The expense certainly was great', observed Francis Douglas drily, 'but it was out of time for Mr Gordon to object to it'.

Across Schoolhill, almost opposite Robert Gordon's College, is the Schoolhill Viaduct, where a flight of stone steps leads down to the Denburn, now a dual carriageway catapulting traffic down towards the Green and the railway station. From Schoolhill, you look south to the Union Bridge, which carries another endless burden of traffic along Aberdeen's main thoroughfare. If you had been standing on the Viaduct two centuries ago you could have looked down on a less frenetic scene, across the bleachfields in the Denburn valley and down through the arches of the Union Bridge to the old Bow Brig at the foot of Windmill Brae. When it was demolished in 1851 it was 'a briggie wi' age grown grey', but for over a century it carried townsfolk over the Denburn.

Gilcomston Steps today. It runs from the billboards to Woolmanhill.

The Auld Bow Brig was a popular meeting place, but not all the meetings were peaceful. Gangs of Denburn youths known as the Fencibles marched up the Denburn green to the bridge to do battle with the Corbies from Gilcomston. They fought 'wi' stick an' wi' stane till the red-coats cam roun' by the smiddy'. Usually, however, it was a happier scene at the 'briggie'. Boys caught bandies and eels in the burn, farmers met their friends there on Fridays, and souters and tailors gathered to 'hear a' the news' and to sort out the ills of the world:

> In their nichtcaps and aprons the carls wad chat,
> For some wad hae this an' some wad hae that –

Nae political question or Frenchman's intrigue
But was settled an' solved at the Auld Bow Brig.

There was a time when you looked across the Union Terrace Gardens and the Denburn and admired the steeples and spires that rose like sentinels over the rooftops of the town. That famous skyline can still be seen, but now one lofty spire rises starkly above the rest, catching your eye . . . the red-brick Triple Kirks spire, waiting for its death sentence. It is just about all that is left of what Lord Cockburn called 'a rude Cathedral-looking mass containing three Free Churches'. The hall of the east church was turned into a restaurant, but efforts to sell the spire as part of a commercial development were unsuccessful. The site became an ugly blot on the landscape, and arguments raged over whether or not Archibald Simpson's masterpiece should be demolished or restored. A big poster on a wall offered space in a six-storey commercial development with parking space for 121 cars. But the years slipped away and nothing happened.

The Triple Kirks were built in 1843 on the site of the School Hill Factory, a notorious cotton factory at the corner of Belmont Street. Old photographs show a number of pantiled cottages huddled together on a steep slope immediately to the north of the Triple Kirks. The cottages, which were occupied by handloom weavers working in the factory, were built on either side of a rough road sloping down to the Denburn and linking it with Schoolhill. 'They sat about in a higgledy-piggledy manner as if they had been built in the Schoolhill and had slid down the brae', said one report. 'They were all shapes and sizes, gable-ends and outside stairs being their most conspicuous features'. This 'break-neck brae', as it was called, was known as the Mutton Brae.

Throughout most of its history the Mutton Brae was regarded as a slum. Certainly, the area around it was riddled with the kind of closes and backyards that became festering sores on the face of the city in the 18th and 19th centuries. It was said that these 'odious-looking "rickles"' disfigured the area. As for the factory itself, it was said to be a hot-bed of vice and sorrow.

The Mutton Brae was the haunt of some very odd characters. William Buchanan, who wrote about them in the *Aberdeen Free Press*, wondered why this corner of the town attracted such people. He thought it might have been the Mutton Brae's isolated position. One of the characters gloried in the name of Beau Aiken. Despite his name, he was no dandy. He wore 'not very clean stockings' on his feet and a Kilmarnock nightcap on his head, and he seemed to want to face both ways at the same time, dressing himself in *two* coats, one in front and one behind. Beau, who was a shoemaker to trade, died about 1820. The first house on Mutton Brae was built in 1749 by a blacksmith called George Smith. When work began on the Denburn Railway in 1863–67 the lower part of the brae was swept away and the building of the Rosemount viaduct in 1885–89 wiped out the rest of it.

The Triple Kirks spire.

Where the Viaduct overlooks the Upper Denburn, hemmed in by towering tenements, you look down on a scene that bears little resemblance to what was there a century ago. The ghost of John Jack haunts this great hollow. He was a 'manufacturer at Gilcomstone', who in 1758 feued out the west side of the brae that climbed up past Blair's Lane to the mill at the top, driven by the Denburn water. It was John Jack who gave his name to the brae, the other side of which was feued out by Alexander Cushnie. Modern flats now stand on Cushnie's side, but the land left vacant by demolition on Jack's side lies unused.

Early this century, the Lower Denburn, the Hardweird, Jack's Brae, Leadside Road and Short Loanings were almost all that remained of the old

Jack's Brae.

Gilcomston. In 1910 the houses were still standing, but most of them were uninhabitable. Nevertheless, these ruinous buildings, particularly those in the Hardweird, provided a glimpse of what it was like in the old slum-ridden days. The Hardweird ran from the steeply-sloping Jack's Brae to Skene Row, a lane that linked it to Skene Street. Skene Row, which ran behind Skene Street School, was originally known as Swine's Close. The name is said to have come from the pigs that crofters drove down this path to the Denburn, but some said it had more to do with its unsavoury reputation.

Davie Duncan knew the Swine's Closie. He had friends in the Hardweird and often played with them 'on the stone staircase that ran down from Skene Street to the Knight Templar's wallie at the bottom'. This was St John's Well,

Patagonian Court, one of the few old courts still existing in Aberdeen.

which stood at the junction of Skene Row and Hardweird, where a steep footpath went down to the Denburn. When Rosemount Viaduct was made in 1855 the footpath was replaced by the stone stairway mentioned by Davie and the well was shifted to the bottom of it.

The Hardweird had been partly demolished when Davie knew it. Most of the houses there had forestairs. Davie called them an 'ailing, ancient pile of mortar and stones, harbouring inside them human beings huddled together in dark holes described as 'rooms''. The children ran around bare-footed, some of them without proper clothing. Huge multi-storey flats look down on the Upper Denburn now, blotting out the memory of what Davie Duncan called 'the menial parade of tenements and dinghy shops' where he was born. His birthplace was a dilapidated house at 113 Skene Street, but his mother left there to stay at 2 Minister Lane, where the access was by a close in Skene Street. Their rooms looked on to Minister Lane and Kidd Street, a narrow street which ran from Summer Street to Chapel Street.

When I wandered through this part of the town, with its skyscraper flats soaring above the Denburn, I was thinking of the man they called 'the ten commandments on two legs'. He was an Irish minister by the name of Dr James Kidd. Called to Gilcomston Chapel of Ease in the late 18th century, he became a legendary figure. No Aberdeen minister, it was said, ever had such a hold over his people or left such a vivid and lasting impression on them – the godly Dr Kidd, they called him.

Aberdeen was a young town then. Its main streets were Castle Street, Broad Street, Gallowgate, Guestrow, Shiprow, Netherkirkgate and the Green. Beyond them were cornfields and vegetable gardens. 'You could have gone from end to end of it before breakfast and not suffered any inconvenience', commented one writer, adding: 'Unless from the odours'. Union Street was no more than a dream. There were no policemen and no cabmen, and only one stage coach linked the town with the outside world. There was only one newspaper, the *Aberdeen Journal,* published once a week, price 7½d.

Although no more than 5ft. 10in. in height, Dr Kidd was a giant of a man, massively built, with a large head, a broad chest, and a deep, strong voice that boomed out majestically from his pulpit. He always wore a long, loose greatcoat resplendent with brass buttons, along with knee breeches and black silk stockings. When he grew old and bothered with gout, he slipped on woollen stockings beneath the silk ones to keep his legs warm.

He was a magistrate as well as a minister and his symbol of office was a big, old-fashioned umbrella. He used it like a sword, whacking and striking at anyone found disturbing the peace. The sight of him advancing on wrongdoers with his umbrella raised was enough to make them take to their heels. Hecklers, or flax-dressers, were notorious for their drunkenness, and on one occasion he came across two of them fighting drunkenly at the side of a burn. They were members of his congregation, so he grabbed them both by the nape of the neck, knocked their heads together, and ducked them in the water.

His congregation loved him. They gave him a house in Chapel Street and an old ghillie presented him with a stick said to have belonged to 'Prince Charlie'. Another member of his congregation gave him a pair of silver spectacles because his sight was going. In later years, however, he had his critics, or, at any rate, one detractor. 'Anything in common the local folk had had with Dr Kidd or his religion in my time was never apparent', said Davie Duncan, writing in *Tenements and Sentiments* eighty years after the preacher's death.

It seemed that Davie had reacted to tales of Dr Kidd in the same way that he had reacted to the Grammar School; to him the Gilcomston minister was simply another symbol of patronage and privilege. 'The families that I knew', he wrote, 'were the salt of the earth: the Browns, Websters. Simpsons and Smalls, all of Minister Lane. They gave out of their little, that it hurt. They may not have had the bible in their hands, but they had the fullness of heart that the Lord Jesus preached and practised about his meaning of giving.'

CHAPTER THREE

Privies and Pig-Styes

Aberdeen was a conglomeration of closes, courts, lanes and wynds more than a century ago. Dark passages opened up like festering sores in a town that was 'crowded with buildings and abominably filthy'. But it was no worse than in any other city; Edinburgh was 'abounding in dingy closes and dark stairs', a town where at times it was best to hold your nose. Boswell, walking Auld Reekie's High Street with Dr Johnson, said to his friend, 'Sir, I can smell you in the dark!' There was a verse which summed it up:

> . . . antrim folk may ken how snell
> Auld Reekie will at morning smell

The smell was no less pungent in Aberdeen. 'Malodorous' was a word frequently used in descriptions of the town in the eighteenth and ninetenth centuries. Francis Groome, visiting the city before the publication of his *Gazetteer of Scotland* in 1883, was impressed by the approaches to the city and by Union Street, which he thought 'enchanting'. It possessed 'all the stability, cleanliness and architectural beauties of London's west-end streets'.

But Groome discovered a less-enchanting Aberdeen behind this shining new thoroughfare – a hidden city where poverty and misery walked hand in hand. Before the street was built the town was contained within the old royalty, an area defined by Royal Charter. It was, said Groome, an assemblage of narrow, ill-built, badly arranged thoroughfares without any good openings into the country. Stone houses were 'possessed exclusively by grandees', and even in the mid-eighteenth century wooden houses had formed the west side of the Broadgate. The 'very best streets' were narrow, uneven and paved with cobblestones, and the buildings were abominably filthy. The thoroughfares leading to the North were 'steep, rough, narrow and malodorous'.

Even the new town, apart from its public buildings, was 'rude, irregularly arranged and unsubstantial'. The end of the eighteenth century brought major changes in the city, but, ironically, the new developments worsened the lot of the poorer people. They produced, said Groome, grandeur and meanness side by side. The density of the old royalty was greatly increased by the developments. In the 1880s no fewer than sixty narrow lanes and about 168 courts or closes of an average breadth of at most seven feet still existed – and they were mostly situated in the immediate or near vicinity of fine new streets'.

The average distribution of the inhabitants of St Nicholas stood at as high a ratio as 16.8 to each house. 'Some closes, such as Smith's and Peacock's, adjacent to the east end of Union Street, exhibit the lower grades of civilisation only a few steps from the higher', said Groome. Courts branching off the Gallowgate were said to be 'the dingiest and most unwholesome to be found anywhere in a British town'. The Gallowgate and the Shiprow, once the principal approaches to the city, declined rapidly after the opening up of Union Street. Well-off citizens moved west and their houses became more and more squalid, ending up as 'mere styes for human swine'.

This drift away from the royalty was noted by Dr Alexander Kilgour and Dr John Galen, secretaries of a committee set up in 1840 to inquire into the sanitary condition of the poor in Aberdeen. 'As nearly all families of the better classes have left courts for more airy residences', said their report, 'the character of courts and closes has much fallen. They are occupied by a much inferior description of tenantry than they were some years ago, and much less attention is given to keeping them clean. They are not only ill-ventilated, but they have an open kennel [gutter] running along them which is the receptacle for all sorts of filth'.

Interestingly, Dr Kilgour had a drug shop in the 'unwholesome' Gallowgate and lived above it. Stout and heavily built, he was blunt and kindly in his manner, enjoying life, wining and dining at the Broad Street home of the printer Lewis Smith, along with such literary celebrities as Joseph Robertson and John Hill Burton. They drank toddy and ate Finnan haddocks and giant crab-claws – 'partans' taes' the locals called them – and talked politics. But above all Kilgour was a man with a social conscience. He began his political life by haranguing crowds from a mail-cart on the Aberdeen Links, and his house in the Gallowgate was a meeting place for public-spirited people interested in the town's progress. There can be little doubt that their conversation turned to the state of the overcrowed, poverty-stricken royalty on their doorstep.

Aberdeen was said to be 'fever-haunted' in the early years of the nineteenth century. There were three epidemics over a period of twenty-three years. People spoke fearfully about 'the fever', which was, in fact, typhoid – a disease that was to return and strike Aberdeen more than a century and a half later. The first epidemic lasted from 1817 to 1819, the second from 1831 to 1832, and the third from 1837 to 1840. It was during the third epidemic that Dr Kilgour and Dr Galen drew up their report. It painted a sordid and alarming picture of a city in which the main causes of epidemic diseases were overcrowding, poverty and intemperance.

Houses occupied by the poorer people were generally three storeys high,

The Castlegate, from one of the old closes that can still be seen there.

some with cellars which were inhabited. The glass in the windows of the common staircase was often broken. There were no pipes to carry dirty water from the upstairs apartments down to the gutters or drains, so the water was left until it became putrid. When it *was* carried downstairs it was often spilt.

Landlords overcharged their tenants and squeezed them into as small a space as possible. The accommodation for aged paupers and widows with young families was usually a single garret room, and labourers with wives and families also had to settle for one room. A Dr Keith, giving evidence to the committee, said that crowding was 'fearful'. He had seen six or eight people sleeping in one room, 'with every crevice stopped'. He had more than once been nearly suffocated on entering an apartment when several of them were up. Another witness said that there were several inferior lodging-houses in the district which were crowded with mendicants or vagrants. Here, contagious diseases were always found. Beds which were let to vagrants at a low rate were usually 'kept very dirty' and when someone died a newcomer was put into the bed without any attempt to clean it.

William Cameron, a notorious Glasgow hawker – his nickname was Hawkie – frequently visited Aberdeen. He was taken on one occasion to a condemned house in a notorious court called Sinclair Close, which ran from Justice Street towards the Salvation Army Barracks. The close was known locally as 'Tink-a-loe' and even Hawkie's experience in the flea pits of Glasgow hadn't prepared him for what what he saw there. 'This close contains the rummiest characters Aberdeen can produce', he said.

Although Aberdeen was said to be well situated for effective drainage, there were no large common sewers in the old royalty. The lack of them was made up for by the use of cesspools, mostly carrying rain and surface water and water used in kitchens and water-closets. Ash-pits were also 'remarkably deficient', or were kept in the worst possible order.

Manure was collected by carts every morning from the street doors or the heads of closes. A bell on the dustcart signalled its arrival, but householders often didn't bother to put their ashes at the head of the court for collection. The filth was retained in the house till it had 'accumulated past endurance'. Then, more often than not, it was simply thrown out into the court, forming an open dunghill.

The report went on: 'In examining some of the most densely-peopled streets and those where the courts are most numerous, the proportion of receptacles for filth is far below what it should be. The Gallowgate, a street containing forty-four courts, with an average of four houses in each, has only seventeen ash-pits and ten privies. North Street (West North Street) with numerous courts and densely peopled by a very low class, has only twelve receptacles for filth and not one privy.'

So it went on . . . a depressing tale of overcrowding and lack of sanitation.

The shortage of public lavatories meant that the bye-streets and lanes, as well as the courts, were usually 'exceedingly filthy'. Even the Denburn, with its water cascades laid out in ornamental style, was an open sewer. 'Into this ornament of the town', said the report, 'there falls above forty-five drains, kennels or common sewers, and at one part it is the recipient of all the filth from some low houses in the vicinity.'

The Harbour was even worse. All the sewers and drains of the town poured their effluent into it. The result was that it was covered with a thick, fetid mud, which at low water became coated with bubbles of a noxious gas. This gave out 'a most intolerable stench that is perceived at a considerable distance in the town'. Aberdeen has suffered from many 'pongs' over the years, but nothing could ever have matched the awful stink that rose from the harbour back in the early 1800s.

Life in Aberdeen at that time was recalled in a book, *Memories of Two Cities, Edinburgh and Aberdeen,* written by Professor David Masson, a graduate of Aberdeen University, who became Historiographer Royal for Scotland. The book, which was published in 1911, recalled the old Royalty as it had been in the 1820s before 'the noble length of Union Street' had been completed. Wandering through the town looking at the street names, he was able to pick out 'the remaining skeleton' of the old burgh as it had been in the nineteenth century.

The Windmill Brae, the Green, Huckster Row, the Ship Row, the Justice Port . . . these were among the names that he remembered. Some of the streets were still useful thoroughfares, others were 'hideous in the squalor into which they had degenerated', and one or two were 'doubly hideous from the effects of moral putridity at the mouths of their ugliest and narrowest courts'.

The language of the street appalled him. 'To go through Justice Port', he said, 'even in the daytime, was to hear within one or two minutes full excerpts from the foulest wealth of anatomical and physiological words known to the British vocabulary; and even Justice Port was as nothing compared with one long narrow lane called the Vennel, in whose double row of ghastly houses, their windows stuffed with rags and old hats, brutality was more quiet only because more murderous.'

The Vennel, originally called Gordon's Wynd, ran from the Gallowgate to Lochside and took its name from the French *venelle*, meaning a narrow mean street. G. M. Fraser, in his *Aberdeen Street Names,* said that a vennel had become associated throughout Scotland with 'any place which is so particularly mean and squalid that it might be termed a pig-stye'. The Aberdeen Vennel was cleared away in 1842 to make way for St Paul Street.

The 'moral putridity' mentioned by David Masson seeped through the town like an obnoxious, unstoppable tide. Masson's repugnance at the foul language was shared by William Skene, who wrote a series of articles for the *Evening*

Express dealing with life in the east end of the city between 1840 and 1860. One of the worst areas was Castle Street and around the Justice Port, a favourite meeting place of criminals and down-and-outs – men and women from 'the lowest dens about Smith's Court, Peacock's Close, Pensioner's Court and the adjacent lanes and wynds. Their language, said Skene, was 'simply appalling'.

It was not uncommon on a fine summer afternoon to see twenty or thirty of them sitting or lying on steps leading up to the old Record Office at the top of Castle Street. A police patrol would come along and clear them off the footpath, but whenever the 'bobbies' were past they would settle down again. The Record Office was built in 1779. The ground floor was the sheriff clerk's department and the upper floor was used for 'meetings of the county gentlemen'. It also housed the library of the Society of Advocates until the Advocates' Hall was built at the corner of Back Wynd and Union Street.*

The Record Office moved to King Street in 1833, but the old office carried on for long after that. It was finally removed in 1891 when Justice Street was widened. At the same time, many old lanes were swept away. 'Their names have vanished along with their evil memories as slums of the vilest character – the Cowgate, Mauchline Tower Court, Bothwell's Court, etc.', wrote Robert Anderson, in *Aberdeen in Bygone Days*.

Bothwell Court, which was at 25 Justice Street, was named after Baillie George Bothwell, a candle manufacturer. The Baillie himself complained to the magistrates about the number of 'dissolute females' who congregated in Park Street, Justice Port, and the north end of Castle Street. When householders sent their servants out they were met with a barrage of 'indecent and blasphemous language'. Mason's Court was one of the black spots; it was entirely occupied by prostitutes. The woman who owned the property said they had literally taken possession of the premises.

One councillor said that a great many beggars with sore arms and legs were to be seen lying about the streets. It was, he said, 'a disgusting sight'. When the Provost was told about this state of affairs he blamed the Police Comissioners. If he had his old friends, Charlie Clapperton and Simon Grant, he said, he would soon put such nuisances down. Clapperton and Grant were well-known town serjeants.

Nothing was done about the problem until George Stirling, a local grocer and a Police Commissioner, took the law into his own hands. Stirling bought property in Nailer's Court, at the back of the Salvation Army Barracks, only to find that it was full of squatters. When they refused to move he had the windows and doors removed. That didn't work, so he sent for a water hose and turned it on the uninvited 'guests'. 'Amid the shouts and yells of all the

_____

*Now in Concert Court

The Bool Road and its theatre. 'One Penny Only', says the sign at the entrance. Top-hatted drunks dance in the street, a man holds out a whisky bottle from a window, and two men are involved in a punch-up.

gamins in the district', it was reported, ' the poor wretches fled like a lot of half-drowned rats'. After that, the building was barricaded until it could be demolished and new premises built.

Down-and-outs and prostitutes could be seen sitting in groups of half-a-dozen or so all the way from the Record Office down to Albion Street. Albion Street, which ran from the junction of Justice Street and East North Street to the Links, was originally known as the Bowl or Bool Road because it led directly to a bowling green. At one time it was a main thoroughfare leading out of Aberdeen to the north. No one is quite sure why the name was changed, but it was probably because of its reputation. It was said to be 'the most debased and neglected part of the city, a special haunt of dissipation, a very hotbed of profligacy and vice'.

Here, people flocked to the Bowl Road Theatre, which was not so much a centre of culture as a den of iniquity. It was called the Penny Rattler because a penny was charged for admission. An old sketch of the Bool Road shows a large sign above the theatre entrance reading 'ONE PENNY ONLY'. Men in lum hats are seen cavorting drunkenly outside the entrance, while a cloth-capped theatre-goer is lashing out with his fist at another man. Women sprawl

The view up Union Street from Marischal Court. The area in the bottom left-hand corner, behind the Salvation Army Citadel, was once a meeting place for drunks and down-and-outs.

about on the pavements, a scraggy mongrel sniffs at a fish basket lying in the street, and a man leans out of a window waving a bottle of liquor.

'All the female black-guardism of the district' could be found in the area near Albion Street. But as well as parading their wares openly in the streets, prostitutes did a lively business in the local brothels. There were some notorious madames in the city. Meg Dick ran an infamous house known as 'The White Ship', said to be one of the most notoriously patronised brothels in the city. It was situated in Park Street and in 1816 it was looted and burned by an infuriated mob, who hauled its furniture out into the street, piled it high, and burned it to ashes. After this outburst of violence seven men were arrested and put on trial before the Circuit Court.

Salmon Meg, another well-known brothel-keeper, also faced the wrath of the mob. Meg, who was said to be 'a fine specimen of flesh and blood', ran a brothel at the junction of the Netherkirkgate and Dubbie Raw. When the mob broke down her door with a blazing tar barrel she escaped through a back window and took shelter in St Nicholas kirkyard. The incident gave rise to a song which went:

The Castlegate, with Simpson's Restaurant in the background and the Town House spire behind.

She sat on her creepie, and dreadin' nae harm,
Was thinkin' how a'thing wad gang at the term,
When a mob wi' tar barrel cam' doon by the door
An' play'd her the tune o' 'Lochaber no more'.
O, Stumpie, the lawyer, O, Stumpie, the laird,
They hae ta'en awa' Maggie, aside the kirkyard.

Stumpie was William Kennedy, the city analyst. Why he was featured in the song was never made clear, but accusations of impropriety were flung around indiscriminately in the early years of the 19th century. He may have been linked

Another view of the Castlegate.

with them. George Walker, in his book, *Aberdeen Awa'*, said that if you could peep through a half-opened door into the highest circles of society in the city in 1813 you would be thankful that you lived at the end of the century and not at the beginning.

'Vice reigned rampant and defiant of all restraints', he wrote, 'flaunted itself in public, jostled and insulted decent citizens in the open streets and unblushingly braved morality and public opinion in houses which became notorious. The inmates of these houses made direct and unconcealed attacks on the character of many of the most respected citizens in the hope of hush money, and blackmailing afterwards if they found a weak victim'.

He told the story of a police court hearing in which the presiding Bailie asked a witness – a brothel keeper – where she resided. 'Weel, yer honour, ' she said.

'Ye needna ask that, for mony's the time ye've been in my house!' The Baillie indignantly denied it. 'If it wasna you', said the woman, 'it was your son Jock – he's a good customer and yer jist as like ither as twa peas!'

This, then, was the ugly face of Aberdeen nearly two centuries ago, the city where, as G.S. Fraser put it in his poem *Lean Street*, the foul rain rained on poverty. The coming of the twentieth century brought great changes; the city continued to push outwards, and the old royalty gradually disappeared. The closes vanished one by one. Today, only a handful remain. Oddly enough, the most prominent survivor is Peacock's Close in the Castlegate. It was named after Francis Peacock, the nimble-footed dancing master who made the town's bailies dance to his tune. He lived there before it became one of the dingiest and most disreputable alleys in the town.

As far back as 1850, feuars and proprietors petitioned the police commissioners to have the name changed. It had, they said, fallen into such disrepute that the very name was sufficient to deter many respectable parties from taking houses in that quarter. The board, surprisingly, turned down the request.

More than half a century later, G.M. Fraser was forecasting that Peacock's Close would 'soon be a thing of the past'. The old crowded tenements running along one side of it had nearly all been abandoned and other properties would be pulled down. Because of its historical interest, he thought there would be regret that the clearance 'would soon obliterate a street name that has continued the memory of a most worthy citizen to this day'. But Peacock's Close still stands, and it is unlikely that anyone will now cock a snook at history and have it torn down.

CHAPTER FOUR
Age of Eccentrics

John Black, Boot and Shoe Maker. Dealer in Old Boots and Shoes, and Repairer of Shoes on reasonable terms, Letter-writer on any subject to any part, and no charge made, returns his grateful thanks to his Friends and the Public in general for their liberal support. Old Boots and Shoes bought and sold.

23 Justice Street, Aberdeen. Aug 9, 1839.

Fourteen years after John Black, Dealer in Old Boots and Shoes, opened his shoemaker's shop in Justice Street, he printed the above advertisement and distributed it to his customers. It was a 'thank you' from a souter whose talents and interests went far beyond mending tackety boots. He was also a preacher and a teacher – and the man who discovered a new and profitable way of bringing newspapers to the people.

John Black, six feet tall and impressively dressed, was well known in the Castlegate area. When he changed his shoemaker's apron for outdoor clothes he wore a surtout coat, a white waistcoat, and a 'chimney-pot' hat, but, curiously, he never wore stockings. He always had an ivory cane in his hand. His house had its gable to the street and his shop door was divided into two halves like an old-fashioned 'smiddy' door. He was often seen leaning over one half, chatting with the mill girls and gossiping with the neighbours.

Brought up in the Gallowgate, he served his time as a shoemaker and in 1825 started up in business on his own. His work-a-day clothes were almost as striking as his 'full dress'. He sported a soldier's cocked bonnet (his father had been an Army sergeant) and a white shirt, and his leather apron stretched down from his chin and over his ample belly to his 'never-to-be-forgotten bauchles'. As well as mending old boots in his shop, he wrote letters for illiterate customers.

John was a religious man. He held prayer meetings and Sunday School classes in what was known as John's Hall, which was nothing more than a shed with a tiled roof and an earthen floor covered with sawdust. The hall was also a museum, for John was an avid collector. He sometimes bought items that were highly suspect – like the cocked hat said to be worn by Lord Nelson at the Battle of Trafalgar. His prize possession was a letter from Prince Albert's secretary thanking him for a gift of a pair of Wellington boots he had sent to the Prince.

But it was in the newspaper business that John made his name. He started a scheme known as 'Passing Round Papers', letting out newspapers at a charge of a halfpenny for two hours. The idea was that they would be sold to syndicates of four or five people, and then, after they had been read, passed on to other syndicates. His customers included businessmen who were well able to stump up 4 ½ d for their own newspaper, but they preferred the 'passing round' kind. One of his clients was his neighbour, Bailie Bothwell, the candlemaker who made a name for himself by turning a hosepipe on the thieves and prostitutes lazing about in Pensioners' Court near his 'hall'.

William Skene, whose 'East Neuk Chronicles' appeared in the *Evening Express* during 1896, recalled that he was often the messenger who took 'passing round' papers to the readers. 'Some of my relations in the country, within ten miles of the city, used to get the Wednesday's *Aberdeen Journal* on the following Wednesday, and it had not finished its round even then', he wrote. 'In many cases it was passed round till it was almost in tatters'. Another well-known customer was George Black, a druggist, whose shop was in Castle Street, almost at the top of the notorious Peacock's Close. Skene, who collected the paper for John's namesake, described him as a 'masher with well-oiled, dark, curly hair'. He was known as Dandy Black.

In the early 1850s, the *Aberdeen Journal* had a correspondent at Cluny called Gordon, who was something of a poet. Black, who was no great speller, wrote to him, inviting him to 'see my musseem of couriosets without anney charge', and explained how under his syndicate system 'the prencaple Newspapers are given out by me to read at one half pennie per three Hours'. He added that he had 'don so for eighteen years', and asked Gordon to 'make a verse or two' about his work. The result was that a poem by the Cluny poet appeared in the *Aberdeen Journal* praising the souter:

> For John he is crafty, and knows P's from Q's;
> He will barter or bargain, or cobble your shoes,
> At fixing a taebit or driving a tack
> There's none in the trade can compete wi' John Black.
>
> Both reading and writing he nightly doth teach;
> To the sinners around him he hires one to preach;
> A magazine, newspaper, novel, or track,
> Are lent for a farthing an hour by John Black.

The poem went on to mention some of the curiosities in John's museum, among them Nelson's 'cocked hat' and a sword which now rusted in Black's 'peaceful hands', and it described how he raised subscriptions for good causes and organised 'monstre pleasure trips'. In 1858, he contracted typhus fever and died. He was buried in St Peter's Cemetery and a small square granite stone was placed over him. A weeping willow tree cast its shadow over his grave.

John Black, Dealer in Old Boots and Shoes, was a glorious eccentric in an age of eccentrics. He lived in one of the most disreputable areas of the town, a stone's throw from the Castlegate. Before the Poor Law Act of 1845 consigned down-and-outs to the poor's house, a ragged army of vagrants and venders swarmed about the Castlegate, picking up a threadbare living in the best way they could, hawking almanacs, playing the fiddle, singing, selling meat pies, or tempting people with 'dainties'. One of the most notable characters in Aberdeen in the 1830s was a street vender who sold 'dainties'. They were called 'Chelsea Buns', and that was the name given to the man who sold them.

The Castlegate of that time was described in John Ramsay's *Selected Writings*. 'The Plainstanes', he wrote, 'were originally to be used, and were used, as an exchange for the city merchants. There they might have been seen of a fine morning in powdered periwigs and velvet gowns, stately pacing, more like lords than mere merchants. In latter times the place was the favourite promenade of all sorts of lounging loafers, and specially of proudly-strutting recruiting sergeants'.

The fishwives sold their goods on the steps of the Plainstanes – 'real finans and partans at three ha'pence a pair all so sweetly fresh'. Then there were the huxters . . . 'little rosy Betty Osely (Oswald), poor bodie, with her wheel of fortune; or Tom Thumb, an old campaigner, with his cap and its fateful polyhedron, and his vixen spouse; and Gibbery John with his hazardous dice, all so tempting for the youngster with his Friday bawbee'.

Little Betty Osley wasn't the only 'poor bodie' . . . there were plenty of others for whom the wheel of fortune swung in vain. They had names like Moorikan Rum, Ginger Blue, Sawdust Calder and 'Reed' Tappie. Moorikan Rum was said to be the sole survivor of the crew of a Danish vessel wrecked on the Black Dog. The only words he could speak when he was picked up were 'Moorikan Room', which were thought to mean 'American Rum', a drink he probably got when he was at sea. He lived in a hut in the woods of Udny.

Another well-known character was a little old man known as Jumpin' Judas, who earned some coppers by dancing and singing the ballad 'Maggie Lauder' on the Plainstanes. He was once given some cast-off clothing, including a cocked hat. For all we know, it may have been John Black's cocket bonnet, past its best and handed on. At any rate, Judas wore it when he had his portrait painted by a local artist. He then had coloured prints made, sold them, and revelled for a time in his unaccustomed wealth.

The name of one wandering dealer was Quill Charlie. He was a quill dresser, but he had no great skill at the trade and concentrated on hawking quills and steel pens, which he carried around in a carpet bag. He sold them at lawyers' offices and counting houses, but his appearance could have done little for his salesmanship. He had a low forehead, bleary eyes (no eyelashes), a huge club-like nose and negro-type lips. He was unwashed, unkempt and unshaven, with a battered hat and threadbare clothes, and when he eventually gave up selling quill pens he took a job as a scavenger. It seemed a kind of poetic justice.

Buttermilk Benjie, Pie Bob, Feel Willie, Dicky Daw, Feel Roddy . . . the nicknames of these forgotten characters pour out from the past. A 'funny crank' of a man who went begging from door to door was called 'Weel-maybe-a-white-hat-winna-eat-and-a-black-hat-winna-chew'. The name was given to him because he was always repeating these words, but nobody knew what they meant. The nicknames may have been cruel and unfeeling, but they were devastatingly accurate. No one had any doubt about how Piddly Guyan got his nickname, or, for that matter, Lang Willie Milne, who had legs as long as stilts. Gurk Middleton was given *his* nickname because 'Gurk' meant a short, fat person.

A common nickname in those days was 'Stumpie', meaning a one-legged man. Sandie ('Stumpie') Campbell was a seaman who had his leg amputated half-way below the knee and hopped about in what he called his 'dot-and-go-one' style, while James Brownie, a paper-ruler, had a wooden leg that they said could be heard stumping about half a mile off. Yet, oddly enough, he was nicknamed 'Snuffie' Brownie, not Stumpie, which may have been because he had a sniffle as well as a stump.

Women also had their share of nicknames. 'Mary wi' the Hat', who lived in the Upperkirkgate, always wore a man's hat because, it was said, she had been jilted by a lover. Another Mary was known as 'Methodist Meg'. Dickie Daw, who had a cast in her eye and a speech defect, went around saying, 'Gie's a bawbee, gie's a bawbee' and was eventually sent to the poor's house. She was said to be 'repulsive-looking and merciless'. There was also a virago called Jean Carr, who didn't have a nickname, but who hated men and carried a big stick to keep them at bay.

Among the street musicians were a number of 'blin' fiddlers' . . . Blin' Johnnie Melven, who lived in the Shiprow and played during the summer season on steamers trading between Aberdeen and Newhaven; Blin' Willie Milne, who made a noise like a 'clockin' hen' while playing the 'Hen's March;' Blin' Johnnie Hogarth, who worked his jaw while wielding his bow and got the nickname 'Chaw-Cheesie', and Blin' John Ross, who was a cut above the rest and had a signboard in the Spital saying 'teacher of the fiddle and player'.

Perhaps the best-known of all the blind hawkers and musicians was Duncan McKinlay, who for some reason or other was known as Blin' Bob. He wasn't a fiddler, but he had a voice that could rattle the window panes in the Castlegate when he sang 'My New Surtout'. He made his living by writing broadsheets and selling them, along with needles, bootlaces and matches. He also wrote verse, mostly scurrilous. In his younger days he sang at feeing markets, or harangued the farm servants about the iniquities of farmers and their tight-fisted wives. He was said to be a misanthrope, disliking people, yet he was the champion of the poor and oppressed.

His attacks on farmers who starved their servants were carefully calculated, He always declared that he couldn't *sell* his broadsheets because they were so libellous, but he went on to say that he could 'sell them a straw for a penny' and give them the broadsheets free of charge, It was an old trick to get round the law – and more often than not the broadsheets turned out to be harmless.

He also used his soap-box oratory for other reasons. He would address his audience for ten minutes, crying out about the poverty and misery of the poor, and then, having got their attention, would swing into his sales spiel: 'Five and twenty 'shewing' needles for a half-penny, four bootlaces for a penny, five boxes of matches for a penny, a beautiful cambric handkerchief for a penny ..'.

He could hold his audience for hours, but he always kept a sharp eye open for the main chance. When people were eager for news during the Crimean war he bought a large number of old illustrated papers for next to nothing and sold them as 'the latest news from the war'. When his customers complained that there wasn't any war news in the papers, he replied that the newspapers 'tell't lees' about things and he had as much right to tell 'lees' as they had'. It was, ironically, the newspapers that put an end to his broadsheet publishing. He had to reduce the price of a broadsheet to a halfpenny because of newspaper competition, and when the first evening papers appeared they killed off the broadsheet trade.

Blin' Bob's father had a bookstall in Castle Street and they lived for a long time in Gardener's Lane, later in Pensioners' Court. Blin' Bob – Duncan McKinlay – drank too much in later life, and it affected his health. He died in 1889, having steadfastly refused to go into the poorhouse. Perhaps he was remembering the attacks he had made on the poorhouse inspectors in some of his soap-box orations. He was in the streets selling his wares till within two days of his death.

Thousands of people turned out to his funeral on March 8, crowding the Guestrow, Broad Street, Netherkirkgate and St Catherine's Wynd, while Union Street from the Shiprow to Belmont Street was lined with people. Half an hour before the funeral, a number of Duncan's cronies gathered in his house at No. 16 Guestrow. The coffin lay on a table fronting the window. It carried a plain and unpretentiosus inscription – Duncan Campbell McKinlay, aged 70 years.

Despite the city merchants who paraded on the Plainstanes in their powdered periwigs and velvet cloaks, the human flotsam and jetsam that hung about the Castlegate in Duncan McKinlay's day gave it an unenviable reputation. Yet there was another side to the coin. William Skene, who was one of Blin' Bob's closest friends, provided a glimpse of it in his sketches for the *Evening Express*. He wrote about worthies like Maggie Brown's father, whose strident cries sounded out through the streets: 'Fresh mussels! Caller mussels!' and about a vender called Hardacre who had 'a fine musical voice'. Then there was a little wizened-face man selling china – 'Cheen-ey, oh-h!' – with a basket on his arm and a jug he carried as a specimen of his work.

Skene wrote with warmth and understanding about many of the strange and often pathetic 'characters' who haunted the Castlegate towards the end of the nineteenth century. Something *was* lost with their going, but on the whole the clearing of the streets by the Poor Law Act was long overdue. There was no longer room for the Jumpin' Judas's and the Dicky Daws. 'The present generation', declared Skene, 'could have no conception of how town and country was formerly over-run with beggars. Begging was a sort of regular profession all over the land. Every beggar carried his or her meal bag – 'blaw bag' it was called – and I have seen them, times without number, coming into the city laden with meal and potatoes. Part of the meal was given to the lodging-house keepers for lodgings and the remainder sold to small shopkeepers'.

With the turn of the century the Castlegate cast off its old image. Its greatest period was probably after the First World War, when crowds of Aberdonians flocked to the 'Castler' for the Rag Fair, which began on Friday, when stalls sold second-hand clothes and household goods. On Saturday the fruit and vegetable stalls opened up.

May Thomson, a well-known local librarian, recalled these days in a series, 'The Way We Were', which I ran in the *Evening Express* in 1979. 'The stalls, gaily lit by paraffin flares, added to the excitement', she wrote. 'Music would come from all directions, including the Salvation Army Band. There were pipers, accordion players, and Peter, the fiddler, who was a first-class player, and could play anything for a penny'.

Drunken Troupie had a fruit and vegetable stall near the top of Marischal Street, and being Saturday night, his wife and daughter had charge of the stall while he went around shouting, 'Ingans hard and dry, and so am I, all the way from the Holy Land'. His moustache, said May, always looked sodden with drink.

Bronco, a coloured quack doctor, pulled teeth with his bare fingers and 'Professor' Timpson, in his old frock coat and battered tile hat, sold sixpenny tins of corn cure. His own feet were so bad with corns that he could scarcely walk from the Corporation Lodging House to the Castlegate. The markets came to an end when a loop line for tramways was laid around the Castlegate.

The 'Castler' also had its Duncan McKinlays in those days, political orators like Albert Percival Gow, who attacked the police, the council, the wicked capitalists, the Press, almost anyone who came within range of his vitriolic tongue. He had a field day when the *Evening Express* gave a front page spread to the death of King George V. The *Evening Express* was too quick off the mark – the King was still alive! Another soap-box orator who held forth about the capitalist oppressors was fiery little Fraser Mac – Councillor W. Fraser Macintosh. During the General Strike there were street battles at the docks and in Union Street, where attempts were made to halt lorries and trams being moved by so-called 'scab' labour. Bob Cooney was one of the leading 'Commies' in the city – he now has a street named after him.

Up till the outbreak of war there were still a number of 'characters' going the rounds in Aberdeen, singing or playing in the streets or the backies . . . Twang, with his grubby coat tied with string, dancing and playing his 'mouthie' . . . 'Fool Friday', selling his hot-chestnuts . . . Highland Jimmy, playing his accordion, or trying to . . . and a few more nameless street entertainers. But they were singing their swan-song. When the war came they had vanished, never to return.

That colourful, raucous, often riotous era belongs to the past, leaving only a few fleeting memories and, sometimes, a sigh of nostalgia. I can remember hearing the boom-boom of the Salvation Army Band on a Sunday morning as I lay in bed as a boy. I still remember the story of Jeannie, a Castlegate character, who was so impressed by the band that she gave £5 to it. The 'Sally Ann' lass with the collecting box was delighted. 'You can have any hymn you want!' she said. Jeannie thought for a minute, looked at the band, and said, 'I'll tak' *him* wi' the trumpet.'

CHAPTER FIVE
Sixteenth of a Parson

A berdeen was once a town with houses 'so chokingly close to one another, and so abominably filthy, that it was difficult to believe that they could ever be free from pestilence'. Its throughfares were so steep, rough and suffocating that people 'thought it a penance to go through them'.

That grim picture of eighteenth-century Aberdeen was splashed across the pages of the grandly-named *Imperial Gazetteer of Scotland,* a massive two-volume 'Dictionary of Scottish topography', published in London and Edinburgh. The disturbing state of affairs described by the Gazetteer lingered on into the nineteeth century.

In those far-off days it was also a nameless city. There were no street signs to show you the way through those 'suffocating' alleys. A scattering of street names began to appear in the second half of the eighteenth century, put up in a haphazard fashion by the town council and private feuars. There were no commemorative or fanciful names as there are today; they were simply descriptive names – Causeway-end, for instance, indicated the end of the causeway, and Gallow-gait was the 'gait' or way to the gallows. The Cow-gait, a name seen in most Scottish towns, showed drovers how to get to common grazing grounds.

In 1795, the passing of the Aberdeen Police Act brought about the systematic naming of streets – and the numbering of houses. This had to be done 'at the expense of the possessors', and as well as paying for the street signs householders were warned that if they destroyed, pulled down, obliterated or defaced the signs they would be fined the sum of twenty shillings sterling.

The man largely responsible for the naming of streets was John Ewen, a Commissioner with the Police Board. Ewen, who ran a jeweller's shop in the Castlegate, was noted for his public work, but was never universally popular. He was said to be 'a man of polished manners – free, easy and polite, so gentlemanly', and he had an 'inoffensive wit' and a fine taste in literature. On the other hand, he was also an incurable nosey-parker – 'a busybody to the backbone'.

His friendship with the aristocracy (the Duke of Gordon and the Marquis of Huntly were among his customers), brought sneers about his humble

McCombie's Court. Baillie Thomas McCombie, the man who gave his name to it, wanted it paved with flagstones.

background. His father was said to be a wandering tinker and Ewen himself travelled about the countryside as a packman, selling buckles, sleeve-buttons, penknives and other bits of bric-a-brac. Then he began to learn Latin at the age of thirty and went into business.

He was said to be the Father of the Aberdeen Police Act, which was intended to 'improve the Streets, Lanes and other Publick Passages of the City' and to provide better paving, lighting and cleansing. It took years before the numbering of houses was completed. John Gordon, a local painter, was given the job of painting the street names. Later, his son, George, took over from him, but landed in trouble for painting 'improper names' in several streets and lanes. Shore Lane appeared as Custom House Lane, Park Street as Hall Street, and Loch Street as Donald Street.

So, as the city grew, street signs sprouted on its granite walls. As the years rolled on new names appeared and feaurs racked their brains for names of distinction . . . Cromwell, Gladstone, Carnegie and Beaconsfield went up on the walls. No provosts were honoured in this way in those days; the city's civic leaders had to wait till the twentieth century for that to happen. The first was James R. Rust, whose name is recalled by Provost Rust Drive. His work in the civic chair from 1928 to 1932 was said to have added a memorable page to the burgh's history. Others included Provost Watt, Provost Fraser, Provost Graham, and Provost Norman Hogg, who got a Court in Balnagask named after him.

But some people wondered why there was never a Tommy Mitchell Drive, named after the couthy baker-provost who led Aberdeen through the war years, or an Alex Collie Road for the provost who made the city's parks bloom, or a Stephen Crescent as a tribute to the poet-provost, George Stephen, who hawked his verse around the streets where I lived. His provost's lamps still stand outside his old house in Bonnymuir Place, making passers-by think of his poem, 'When the Nichts are comin' doon', or another similar poem, 'The Day's on the Turn' – 'When the days are lenghtenin' oot, man, it mak's the hert cheery to think the warst's past and the day's on the turn.'

I have always had a picture in my mind of a group of solemn councillors sitting in a smoke-filled room in the Town House discussing the latest street names. Of course, there would be a Councillor Swick* there, arguing the toss with his pal Eddie, who was always in a minority of one. They would have long, earnest conversations about names like Boa Vista – 'Na! na! Eddie, that's too Rubislaw Den' – or Ivanhoe – 'There's a picture on at the Virgin Cinema aboot him' – and in years ahead people would wonder how on earth our City Fathers ever came up with such names.

There have certainly been some very odd names over the years, including Boa Vista Place, which runs off the Spital, and three Ivanhoes – Place, Road and Walk – as well as a Bodachra Road at the Bridge of Don and a Midchingle Road at the harbour. There were Midchingle fishings at one time.

Aberdeen's city librarian, George M. Fraser, said that even in our street names we had a certain heritage which we ought to guard carefully. 'There is character, as well as history, in our street names', he wrote. 'They reveal to us a succession of sober-minded earnest people, not given to pretence or display, or seeking distinction much, whose quiet courage and patience are still, and by nature must be for many years to come, foundation qualities of our

---

*Councillor Swick's cartoon by Buff Hardie and Steve Robertson appears in *Leopard Magazine*.

McCombie's Court – the flagstones are still there today.

character'. Whether or not Boa Vista and Ivanhoe say anything about our character depends on your viewpoint, but in his *Aberdeen Street Names* Fraser left out 'nearly all fanciful and high-sounding names'. They were, he said, of no historical value.

From 1800, following the building of Union Street, King Street and George Street, there were new streets almost every year. In 1824, five Aberdeen booksellers decided that what the town needed was a street directory. It was launched in 1825 – a small, paper-covered booklet of about 100 pages containing the names of some 3,500 people. The directory was compiled by Jonathan Cumming, a teacher, who lived in Lamond's Court, off Upperkirkgate, and James Murray, a clerk, who lived in George Street. The price was 2s 6d. and readers dipping into their pockets for a half-crown were warned that 'in a work of this nature perfect accuracy is not to be expected'.

The *Aberdeen Censor*, a weekly newspaper said to be a cut above the majority of popular papers at that time, carried a review of the *Aberdeen Directory*. It said that no book conveyed a greater supply of useful and entertaining ideas than a directory. It contained 'hundreds and hundreds' of Smiths, Milnes and Thomsons (in fact, 97 Smiths were listed) and it also pointed out that on each page there was an average of 'four publicans, three lawyers, two doctors, three-fourths of a midwife, and one-sixteenth of a parson'. It demonstrated, said the *Censor*, that Aberdeen was a drinking, litigious, fighting, child-begetting, merry, religious sort of a place'. What the one-sixteenth of a parson thought about the drinking, fighting and child-begetting is not recorded.

Aberdeen's place in the world of shipping was mirrored in the long lists of shipbrokers, rope and sailmakers, shipbuilders, shore porters and shipmasters. The names of no fewer than 160 ships' captains were given in the directory. These were the men who, as the Aberdeen *Evening Express* commented, 'licked creation' in the famous Aberdeen clippers and were acknowledged in ports in all parts to be 'the best seamen in the world – big, sturdy, strong men who knew their work and could do it'. Then there were the whalemen, who went off to the icy Arctic seas in the hope that they would come back with 'a ship that's fu' o' oil, my lads, and money to our name'. Two of Aberdeen's most famous whaling skippers, Captain William Penny and Captain John Parker, were in the *Aberdeen Directory*.

The old seafarers liked their grog. It was said that there was a public house or hotel for every ship belonging to the port – 130 vintners in all, mostly situated near the harbour. Besides the vintners, the directory listed keepers of inns, hotels and porter and ale houses. The selling of drink was said to be a go-as-you-please business. If you sold pure liquor you were a vintner and if you could let out a bed or two you were classed as an innkeeper. On top of that there were the spirit merchants, and if you had a sudden thirst you could always get a gill of whisky from Jamie Cumming in the ship chandlery down at Footdee.

Fittie did well in the drink trade. For some reason or other most of the public houses at that time were run by women. Blin' Annie Nicol had a pub in Wellington Street and a few doors away was a howff run by Widow Sword, who was known as Lucky Sword. There were two other Lucky's nearby – Lucky Still and Lucky Anderson in York Street – and there, too, you could buy drink at Miss Leslie's grocery.

The keeper at the Pilots' Tavern was Jane Smith. Jane, better known as Jinsie, had her own ideas on how a public house should be run. She often left her customers to help themselves. She would jump out of bed every morning at half-past five, unlock her front door, and then go back to bed. Her bedroom was within hearing distance of the bar and at six o'clock she would hear the first customer arrriving and cry out, 'Is that you, Jamie Cumming?' Satisfied that it was a familiar voice, Jinsie would tell him to 'Help yersel'.

The first *Aberdeen Directory* had a list of all the streets, squares, lanes, closes and courts in the city. There were 318 entries, including 143 courts, 29 lanes, six closes, five wynds, and three squares. Many of the courts were named after the people who lived in them – Daniel's Court in the Castlegate, Farquharson's Court in Schoolhill, Gibb's Court in the Shiprow . . . the list went on and on. Others mirrored local trades and professions; the Plasterers' Court and Candlemakers' Court in the Gallowgate were two of them. There were also names with a more sinister connotation, the Bowl Road, for instance, better known as the *Bool* Road, a vice-ridden area running from Park Street to the Links, and Bridewell Lane, which took its name from a House of Correction in Rose Street. Later editions of the directory threw up new names, among them Headinghill, with its dark reminder of executions and witch-burning on the Castle Brae.

By 1848–49 the list had lengthened and its scope widened. Names and houses were brought together in a format that was to last until the directory ceased publication in 1980. The *Censor* said that the new publication would provide 'a distinct view of the whole place'. Today, more than a century and a half later, it gives a 'distinct view' of an Aberdeen that has vanished. Within these faded pages lies the hidden city . . . a community swallowed up by the past. There are names that no longer exist – Garvock's Wynd, Factory Court, Fisher Row, Knox's Court, Pork Lane, and many more. The ghosts of a forgotten age peer out of the book . . . Mrs Rhind, mantua-maker, 24 Schoolhill; Mrs Ogilvie, sick nurse, 7 Jopp's Lane, Thomas Daniel, stabler, 16 Mealmarket Lane, Matthew Deans, chimney-sweep, 22 Muttonbrae, and the magnificently-named Baron von Paulus Buhl, holding court at No. 14 Dee Street.

Shoemakers and shore porters march through the pages, with coopers and clerics close on their heels, followed by paper manufacturers and pawnbrokers, clerks and coachmen, tinsmiths and tailors, bootmakers and builders, stay makers and straw bunnet makers. Strange-sounding trades and professions leap out at you – cork-cutters, tide-waiters (there were two of them in Brebner's Court), paviers, cowfeeders, nailers who worked in Nailer's Court, heckle-makers, candlemakers, funeral-waiters, smoke doctors, and silk mercers. A tide waiter was a customs officer who boarded and inspected incoming ships, while a heckle-maker was a maker of straw roofs. Dead-houses were mortuaries.

A mercer was a dealer in fine cloths. There were twelve silk mercers in Union Street, including James Gordon, whose shop in the Castlegate was shown in an illustration in the directory. Isaac Mathieson, whose silk mercer's shop was at 33 Union Street, had a hat manufacturer as a neighbour at No. 34. He was the famous Samuel Martin, self-styled Hatter to the People, who fought off his competitors with a publicity and advertising campaign that would have been more in keeping with the 1990s than the 1840s. Sam proclaimed himself to be a *practical* hatter, which, as he said with a sideways glance at Mr Kinnear's hat shop at No. 26, enabled him 'to produce infinitely more stylish and becoming Hats than could be produced at *ordinary* establishments'.

Sam used his advertising columns in the *Aberdeen Herald* not only to sell hats but to pass on to the public his views on everything from the activities of Queen Victoria – 'Three Cheers for our Noble Queen. HURRA! HURRA1 HURRA!' – to the fate of the working classes. He wondered if the Queen might see her way to making him a knight or a peer ('Lord Martin would sound well enough') but it never happened.

In 1904, the *Evening Express* took a look back at the first *Aberdeen Directory*. It marvelled at the peculiar occupations that had been followed by people in the 1820s and had become 'as extinct as the Dodo'. 'We find the name of Caesar Altera, glass blower. Nowadays such a name appearing in the city directory would likely be associated with some Italian restaurant or ice-cream saloon'.

The paper also spotlighted a man who would have been well able to tackle the BSE crisis if he had lived at the other end of the twentieth century. The pioneer of the tinned meat in the industry, it said, could surely be no other than 'Philip James, wine, tea, and spirit merchant, and patentee for preserving in the fresh state all animal and vegetable substances for any number of years'. It also mentioned the 'rather unusual combinations' of jobs held by some citizens. Albert Brown in Justice Street was a 'hosier, billetmaster and jailor', and Peter Wright in the Guestrow worked as an 'ivory turner, musical instrument maker and dentist'.

Knock on any door in this hidden city and you will find a story behind it. Living in lodgings at 11 Bon-Accord Street in 1825 was a Mrs Captain Wade – shipmasters' wives were listed as 'Mrs Captain'. Mrs Wade appeared in the directory fifteen years after her husband, Captain Wade of the steamer *Brilliant*, lost his life while steering his vessel into Montrose harbour during a storm. The steamer gave a heavy lurch, a big sea struck her, and the captain was washed overboard and never seen again. The vessel was driven on to the old South Pier and caught fire, but the passengers and crew were able to scranble ashore.

Mrs Wade's near neighbour at No. 61 was James Giles, R.S.A., who began life as a teacher of drawing. Giles was in his early twenties when he had a studio in Bon-Accord Street. When he died in 1870 about sixty oils and a hundred watercolours were sold in the studio, a dozen of them – Deeside scenes – going to the Queen. Giles is said to have recommended Balmoral to Queen Victoria as a suitable Scottish home.

The Mannie in the Well looks across the Castlegate to the Salvation Army Citadel.

Down at the Castlegate was another painter, 'James Cassie, jun., artist', living at No. 30 Castle Street, now a public house. It was said of Cassie that no one could match him as a marine artist, but to augment his meagre earnings he also painted livestock. There is a story told about how a drunken farmer burst into his Castlegate studio and bawled out, 'Div ye paint nowt [cattle]?' 'Aye!' came the sharp reply. 'D'ye wint yer portrait deen?'

You might also see the portly figure of Ignatius Massie taking the air on the Planestones. He lived at No. 56 Union Street and was listed as James Ig. Massie. He was an auctioneer before becoming manager of the Gas Works and claimed to have found a remarkable echo on the River Dee opposite the Devanha Distillery. His friends lost interest in this great discovery when he took them to the Dee and shouted out, 'What are you doing there?' Back came a voice, 'It's neen o' yer business!'

The *Aberdeen Directory* of 1924 carried the names of only six closes, compared with 143 courts. Burnett's Close commemorated Robert Burnett of Elrick, a merchant and burgess of Aberdeen, and Peacock's Close took its name from the city's famous dancing master, Francis Peacock. There was also a Barnett's Close, which ran from the Guestrow to Flourmill Brae. Black Bull Close was at 4 Huxter Row, where the hucksters or hawkers had their booths. There were three hostelries in Huxter Row – the Crown Tavern, the Rising Sun Tavern and the Lemon Tree Tavern.

The Lemon Tree was at No. 7 Huxter Row, up a small court next to the police office. Its hostess was 'old, couthie, courteous Mrs Ronald', who for fifty years served up creamy Finnan haddocks and magnificent partan claws in her 'quiet, cosy howff'. Police, magistrates and councillors dined at the Lemon Tree – and the clergy. An old poem called 'The Synod' told how 'the clatter of tongues' rang through St Nicholas Kirk when the ministers met at Aberdeen on 12 October, 1813. After the meeting they went to dinner 'digesting their wrongs':

> And now methinks at four I see
> The brethern all in 'Lemon Tree' –
> For here, they fail not to convene
> Round Ronald's smoking hot tureen.

What they served up at No. 39 Loch Street was a different matter. The directory shows it simply as a 'Public Kitchen'. This was a soup kitchen for down-and-outs, who were given a basic diet of a chopin (quart) of barley broth and a large roll of wheaten bread for a penny. There was still a soup kitchen – a restaurant – there until recently, serving food that would have made its nineteenth-century customers smack their lips with relish. The character of the old kitchen was retained, with marble tables gifted in 1894 still being used.

So much for the closes. In those far-off days the courts dominated the crowded area around the Castlegate. Many of them took their names from the people who lived and worked in them. The Gallowgate throws up a number of these 'personal' courts. There were, for instance, two Beatties in Beattie's Court – William Beattie, a builder, and Miss Beattie, a dressmaker, perhaps his daughter, while a Mrs Samuel Duncan lived in Duncan's Court and Jopp and Shand, advocates, had their office in Jopp's Court. There were three Henderson Courts off the Gallowgate – and a fourth in Broad Street. William Rollo, the keeper of the dead house, lived in the Broad Street court.

The old Lochlands was fast disappearing by the end of the eighteenth century (it had completely disappeared by 1838) and a reminder of it is given in an entry in the directory – Salter's Court, 50 Lochside. There is no name with the address, but a salter was someone who salted fish. There is still a Lochside Bar in Loch Street. Another court, Burn Court, took its name from a stream carrying water from the loch into the town. When the city pushed out from the Castlegate, building new streets and new houses, the old courts were snuffed out one by one, like flickering candles, among them the National Bank Court. Only a few are left to remind us of that bygone age.

Shoppers take a short cut from Union Street to the Netherkirkgate through a court that has been there for 184 years. McCombie's Court was named after Thomas McCombie, who was a bailie in Aberdeen at the start of last century. He built a new house in the Netherkirkgate in 1814 and laid out the court at the same time. The directory shows only one householder in McCombie's Court in 1825 – Mrs Buckland, who had lodgings there.

Bailie McCombie didn't only give his name to this Union Street passage, he also made famous a particular brand of snuff. There are no lodgings there now – and no snuff – but it is a busy, well-used alley. When McCombie Court was built the Bailie gave instructions that 'it should be paved with flagstones in the manner of the entry of Rotten Row to Union Street'. Rotten Row was a narrow little street that ran from the Shiprow across the Netherkirkgate into the Guestrow before Union Street was built. It has gone, but McCombie's Court has survived – and its flagstones are still there.

CHAPTER SIX
Shargar Shoppies

Aberdeen's mile-long Union Street has always made the poets reach for their pens. 'The stanie straucht o' Union Street' was how Alexander Scott described it. Ian Crichton Smith told of a time when it was 'an arrow debcouching on crooked lanes where women sweated like leaky walls', while Charles Murray, wilting under the heat in South Africa and dreaming of fishwives selling their dilse and partans in the Market, wearied for 'the wind an' weet an' drivin' drift in Union Street'.

Union Street has been called 'the finest street in Britain, if not in Europe', yet some say that the planners have degraded it, that the Aberdeen architect and historian Fenton Wyness hit the nail on the head three decades ago when he predicted that the city would fall from architectural grace. Now it has become a city of covered-in consumerism, a glittering fantasy world of shopping malls and moving stairways, where you can get everything from hamburgers to *haute couture* without braving the 'wind an' weet' on Union Street. The 'town of pure crystal' has lost its purity. In his poem 'Vandalism', A.M. Davidson looked around and saw only 'caul gless and concrete'.

'Gweed Lord', he cried, 'ye've fair made a sair soss o' *my* Bon-Accord'.

This was the street that Francis Groome said in 1822 had 'all the gaiety and brilliancy' of Paris, but there was little *jeu d'esprit* about it in the closing years of the twentieth century. A different kind of Union Street had begun to emerge, minus many of the 'multiples' and most of the old family stores. The cinemas had vanished . . . the Playhouse, the Majestic, the Capitol, the Picture House, the Regal, the Queen's, all gone. 'Woolie's' once held sway with their 'nothing over sixpence' boast: now McDonald's monster burgers have taken their place. Cars choke the street, pedestrians choke the pavements. Building societies boom. Travel shops hurry you off to faraway places.

Stand on the Union Bridge and the words of A.M. Davidson's poem come drifting down the years – 'Fit's *that* ye hae biggit owre Union Brig?' What they had biggit was a clutter of shops that were to knock Kelly's cats off their pedestals – the cats that Harry Gordon said were spittin' fire at him – and would 'blin' the vista owre by Torry Bay'. Alexander Scott said that the folk who built the shops were 'bonnieness-blind'. Who else, he asked, with only one brig giving open space on Union Street, would 'block thon brichtness out wi shargar shoppies?' Flanking this line-up was C & A's store, which stood at the corner of Bridge Street. The new 'shargar shops' were between it and the Trinity Centre, looking curiously out of place on a bridge whose foundation stone had been laid as far back as 1801.

Yet whatever soss they make of Bon-Accord in the new Millenium, the city's main thoroughfare will no doubt survive. In the first months of 1998, it was as if the voice of the poet Davidson had spoken again – 'Fit's that they're biggin' on the Union Brig *noo*?' The old bridge shops were holding closing-down sales, wooden boardings were going up with posters announcing new developments, and behind them workmen were hammering out two new shops to replace the 'shargar shoppies'. The C & A store had moved to the Bon-Accord Centre, eventually being replaced by a building society office, with a branch of Boots next door, and now, farther to the east, the Ottaker group were opening a new bookshop, linked to an upstairs coffee shop. This was leisure book-buying; sofas were provided, allowing customers to browse over the latest best-sellers. Meanwhile, HMV were opening a large music store which would compete with another music shop nearby. Both new shops were planned as part of an extended Trinity Centre.

Ottakers newest and largest Scottish bookshop looked across Union Street to a bronze plaque placed on the Union Bridge in 1908 to celebrate Art and Literature. Now, ninety years later, it was taking on a new meaning, for beyond Bridge Street, a few hundred yards to the west, yet another new bookshop, John Smith's, was opened in April, 1998. This brought the total number of major bookshops in Union Street to six, maintaining a tradition going back to the late eighteenth century, when there were no fewer than four bookshops in the Narrow Wynd, a small, irregularly built lane leading from Broad Street to Castle Street.

History swirls around the turbulent Union Terrace junction. In February, 1805, 'a gentleman on horseback' clip-clopped his way into the pages of the *Aberdeen Journal* when it was reported that he had been permitted to leave the town by riding over the new bridge three months before it was officially opened. He could never have known the traffic maelstrom that would follow in his wake a century or so later. In 1914, when King Edward VII, described by the poet Alistair Mackie as 'that fat clort', was being heaved on to his great granite plinth at the corner of Union Terrace, the motor car had taken over.

Behind King Edward, statues paced the length of Union Terrace – the Valhalla of the famous, it was called, although another Aberdeen poet with a jaundiced view of Royalty saw it in a different light. Lewis Grassic Gibbon thought that Edward's statue was 'merely vulgar'. The Prince Consort originally stood – or sat – on the site, although nearer the kerb, but in 1914 Prince Albert had to give way to his son and was moved along the Terrace to Rosemount Viaduct. Meantime, Burns gazed dolefully at his daisy, unaware that one day *his* statue would be dismissed as 'pathetic'.

If Patsy Gallacher, Aberdeen's legendary news vendor, had been around at the time, he would probably have written a bill about it. Patsy, whose stance was at the corner of Union Terrace, often wrote his own news bills, which were generally more interesting than those sent out from Broad Street. He was said to augment his income by supplying regular customers with their French letters, or condoms, as they are now called, slipped discreetly between the pages of the *Evening Express*.

For many years, Pegler's, the fruiterer, was across the street at the top of Bridge Street. George Pegler's shop was originally at the Union Buildings. He advertised his fruit as being 'the cheapest in the market', which wasn't surprising because there were only two fruiterers in the town at the time. Grapes were a luxury enjoyed by the rich, but apples, pears and berries were cheap. Across Bridge Street, next to the Union Bridge, was the elegant Palace Hotel, built in 1874 and burned down in October, 1941. It was one of Aberdeen's most spectacular fires, with breathtaking rescues and heroic fire-fighting. It was thought at first that there was no loss of life, but the following day six charred bodies were found in the debris. It seemed as nothing would ever replace the elegant Palace Hotel, but sixty years later, in the autumn of 1998, a new hotel, Trave Lodge, opened on the upper floors of the Bridge Street-Union Street site.

For generations of Aberdonians the Union Street-Union Terrace junction meant two things – the Mat and the Monkey House. The Monkey House was the Commercial Union building at the corner of Union Terrace, where you met your 'date'. The Mat was the stretch of Union Street where you promenaded on a Sunday night in the hope of *finding* a 'date'. In March, 1962, the Aberdeen librarian Marcus Milne wrote about Union Street in a *Press and Journal* article which carried the headline: 'We walked the Mat and met at the Queen (never the 'Monkey House'!)' 'Union Street has been the "mecca" for the young people of the city since it was laid out in 1800', he wrote. 'When I was young we walked the "mat" and usually met at the Queen. I don't know what name is given to Union Street today but I hear young people speak of meeting at the "Monkey House". Strange that so august a building should be so named.'

Not many people speak about the Monkey House nowadays and the ritual of walking the mat has long since gone. Teenagers still gather there, but now a watchful eye is kept on them by the police. Drugs, muggings and violence have made older people stay away from the city centre on Saturday and Sunday nights. The statue of Queen Victoria at St Nicholas Street was also a favourite meeting place, but when the St Nicholas Centre was built the Queen was moved to Queen's Cross. It was probably what she would have wanted, looking west to her beloved Deeside, but in 1997 it looked as if the planners were still playing chess with the Royal statues. There were rumours that a new park-

Aberdeen's St Nicholas Street in the last century. The pedestal on the right was where Queen Victoria's statue stood before it was moved to the Town House in 1888. In 1893 it was replaced by another statue of the Queen, which was moved to Queen's Cross in 1964. (Courtesy Aberdeen University.)

and-ride scheme would mean another shift for Victoria. Some people thought that she should never have been at St Nicholas Street in the first place, for if a statue was going to be put up there it should have been to the real 'King' of St Nicholas, the man who put this corner of the city on the map – 'Raggie' Morrison.

This is a rags to riches story with a curious twist to it, for the man who made 'Raggie' Morrison famous was named Mearns, not Morrison – and the firm had its origins in a shop run by a spinster called Miss J. Morrison. Miss Morrison's shop was in Black's Buildings, opposite the Woolmanhill infirmary buildings, and it was there that she was joined by her brother William Morrison. an apprentice draper with Lumsden's in Union Street. William did a great deal to build up the success of his sister's business and when the shop was destroyed by fire he opened another one in the Netherkirkgate. From this tiny Kirkgate shop, with a single window in it, the Morrison empire grew and 'Raggie's' legend took wings.

St Nicholas Street in the days of trams and 'Raggie Morrison.

Another young apprentice in the Black's Building shop was James Mearns, who started work in a Broad Street drapery store owned by Baillie Henry Gray, but switched to Morrison's Economic Stores. He was a lad with dreams and ambitions – he wanted to become a sucessful business man and he wanted to buy Aboyne Castle. He did both. He became William Morrison's junior partner, and later joint owner, and it was largely through his enterprise and business sense that 'Raggie' Morrison's became so well-known.

The store's title was designed to attract Aberdonians who were traditionally careful about putting their hands in their pockets. Morrison's *Economic* Stores, said the sign over the door, which meant that you could get a pair of ladies interlock knickers for 6d – 10d and 1/- if you were a big spender. The bill and the money went hurtling round the store in one of those strange overhead pulley wire and cup contraptions that were all the vogue in city stores between the wars. When a bill had to be signed a cry went up, 'Sign B!' summoning Mr Benzie, a Dickensian character with a round red face and steel pince-nez on the point of his nose.

James Mearns was a pioneer of bulk buying and the materials he bought, silk, satins, brocades, bankrupt stocks acquired in his forays all over Britain and into the Continent, were on display at both doors in St Nicholas Street and the Netherkirkgate. You had to move sideways to gain entry, and once through the door you knew by the *smell* that you were in 'Raggie's'. It was like an up-market 'Cocky' Hunter's, the major difference being that the goods were new, of good quality, and priced for the average housewife.

Now 'Raggie's' has gone and Queen Victoria has gone – and St Nicholas Street has gone with them. It is something of a mockery that they have left the old street sign over what is left of St Nicholas Street, a postage-stamp pedestrian area where tramcars once clattered to a halt at the end of their run from Split-the-Win'. The changes removed an awkward bottleneck from a busy corner of the town, but some ageing sentimentalists still sigh for the 'trammies', and for the sight, sound – and smell – of 'Raggie' Morrison's. As the writer Alex Keith once put it, 'there had passed away a monument regarded with veneration by the womenfolk of the North-east, Morrison's Economic Stores, a veritable mine of bargains in good articles for the wise housewife'.

But other memories crowd in as you go up Union Street . . . the *old* New Market, with its fortune tellers, its stalls groaning under a mountain of books, and shadowy cubicles where they were said to offer you services you could never read about in books; the Palais de Danse in Diamond Street, Ernest Bromberg's dance hall, where you tripped the light fantastic to the music of Archie Alexander's band, and, next door, Aberdeen's first News Cinema. Before you graduated to the Palais, Babs Wilson taught you to quick-step and foxtrot in her dance studio farther west, just off Union Street, competing with Madame Murray's, whose young clientele were regarded by Palais dancers as a posher crowd.

Lachlan Mackinnon took a stroll down Union Street in his *Recollections of an Old Lawyer*, which extended over a century and was said to be probably the best book of Aberdeen reminiscences. Union Street, he declared, had become 'the centre of gravity of the city'. He looked back to the time when there were few principal side-streets west of Union Bridge – Union Terrace was a cul-de-sac and there was no Bridge Street – but he could also remember being taken to see Quaglieni's Circus in Bridge Street in 1866, when he was a small boy of eleven.

The old lawyer also wrote about the New Market, where at the foot of the inside staircase he bought partans and finnans from a fishwife called Eppie, who wore a muslin cap and was a 'noticeably handsome married woman'.

Harry Gordon sang a song about 'Eppie, the Auld Fishwife', who sold her wares in the Green. He told the story of how a customer had confronted her and complained, 'Eppie, this ling is no a bit like the piece I got a fortnight ago'. 'Well, it should be', said Eppie, 'it's the same fish'. Had Mackkinon's 'noticeably handsome woman' become the Auld Wife of Harry Gordon's sketch?

In Lachlan Mackinon's childhood, Union Street houses were 'substantial, well designed and comfortable, with ample entrance hall and staircase and spacious rooms'. Decoration usually took the form of green and gold wallpapers and drop-crystal chandeliers, but this style of house decoration gave way in the seventies to subdued dull reds and blacks. There was no bathroom in his father's house and the domestic servants' quarters were dark and cramped. The kitchen had no hot water and above the first floor there was no cold water.

Mackinnon's father, who had a house at No. 233 Union Street, bought some neighbouring property in which the city's first tramway office was housed. At the west end of Union Street, on the north side, a building known as the Water House stored water from the River Dee and distributed it to Aberdeen's 75,000 population. Later, this building was used by William Bain, the cab-hirer who started up a horse-drawn bus service in the city. He had stables and coach-houses behind it.

Lachlan Mackinnon was to play an important part in the development of the city's tramway system. In his *Recollections* he recalled the doubling of the tramway line in Union Street in 1888 and the feud between William Bain and a rival tramway company. Bain objected to the doubling of the track on the grounds that there was too much traffic at the Holburn Street junction and the entrance to his premises would be obstructed. He had a photograph taken showing the junction so crowded with wheeled vehicles that it looked like Piccadilly Circus. Lachlan Mackinnon got the same photographer to take pictures of Bain's men washing their unharnessed cabs at this 'congested' street corner and the line doubling went ahead. Bain bowed out and the tramway company was bought over by the Corporation in 1898.

Queen's Cross was the hub of the tramway system in those early days. Its repair and maintenace depot served the whole city except Woodside until 1896. The depot, which included a body repair shop, a foodstuff facility and a blacksmith's shop, was on the west side of Fountainhall Road, where the Grampian TV studios now stand, and across the street, where the Denburn came gurgling down through open countryside, were the stables. I often louped the burn on a Friday evening before parading with the Lifeboys in Rubislaw Church hall, where we saluted the flag and sang 'Abide with Me'.

In 1887, an ambitious leisure centre was launched behind the tram depot by an Aberdeen lawyer. It included tennis courts, croquet and bowling, a skittle

Queen Victoria on her pedestal at Queen's Cross.

alley – and a skating rink with a cement floor. It was obviously before its time, for in 1883 the project collapsed. The bowling green and tennis courts survived and can be seen on Ordnance Survey maps of 1900, but nothing now remains of that Victorian plan for leisure activity. The owner of No. 1 Queen's Cross, who tried to have Rubislaw Church built of granite instead of sandstone, would probably have been pleased. He was George Washington Wilson, Aberdeen's pioneer photographer.

Queen's Cross and the surrounding area no longer contain the exclusive homes of Aberdeen's elite. Many of its magnificent granite buildings have been turned into hotels and offices. At the turn of the century, Henry Alexander, editor of the *Aberdeen Free Press*, who became Provost in 1932 and was knighted in 1938, lived in GWW's old house at No. 1 Queen's Cross, while another *Free Press* editor, William Watt, lived at 117 Queen's Road. A clutch of medicos also had their homes there, including two Brigade-Surgeons and a Fleet Surgeon, while the J. B. Hegarty, the Postmaster, lived at a house called The Eagles in Queen's Gate.

Five roads converge on Queen Victoria's statue at what many motorists regard as a nightmare roundabout – Queen's Road, Carden Place, Albyn Place,

St Swithin Street and Fountainhall Road. St Swithin Street was originally called South St Swithin Street and Fountainhall was known as North St Swithin Street, but somewhere along the line it was thought that this was confusing and the north section became Fountainhall Road. The man responsible for naming a street after a saint was the Aberdeen advocate Francis Edmond, who owned Kingswells House, but there was nothing pious about his recommendation. It was because he liked a curious poem called 'Legend of St Swithin', written by an Aberdeen bookseller, George Davidson.

George Davidson was known as the 'literary bookseller' of Aberdeen. He served an apprenticeship with a Broad Street bookseller, William Robertson, but decided to find out what lay beyond the literary world. He took a job as a travelling salesman with the Devenha Brewery, which later featured in his St Swithin legend, but eventually returned to bookselling. He had a shop in the old Town House buildings and later in King Street and Union Street. He often wrote for *The Censor,* one of the 'comic' newspapers that were all the rage in the nineteenth century.

It may have been the North-east's dreich weather that inspired his poem, for an introduction to it mentions the frequent flooding in the low-lying lands of Deeside. If there was a shower on St Swithin's Day, July 15, it was almost certain that six weeks of continuous rain would follow. At any rate, the poem was sub-titled 'A Rhyme for Rainy Weather', and the Roman Catholic seminary at Blairs was the place chosen for St Swithin's retreat:

> Saint Swithin was a drouthy saint –
> When in retreat at Blairs,
> He drank a pitcher full of grog
> Before his morning prayers.

Having set himself up for the day, he then drank 'from morn till night', mixing his grog with water from the Dee. This routine came to an end when a scorching drought dried up the Dee and drained the Culter burn. The Sacristan searched everywhere for water, in rivers and lochs, in mill lades and fountains, and in springs and bogs, but without success.

His last hope was the Abbot's fish pond, but this was 'watched with jealous care':

> 'St Swithin!' roared the Abbot,
> 'Fie on the drunken rogue!
> Dares he propose to drain my pond
> That he may swig his grog!
>
> Dares he propose to drain my pond,
> And starve my perch and trout;

'Ho! help – a boat! a boat!' – one of the illustrations from the St Swithin Street rhyme.

Nay! let him take to Bass's Ale
And Devanha double stout.

St Within, regarding the Abbot as a 'stingy sinner', went back to his cell, where he 'wrought some hellish charm'. Next morning, the sky grew black, thunder roared, and the rain fell in torrents. The flooded streams poured through Ballochbuie's woods and down the Garrawalt, sweeping away the Bridge of Ballater, raging over the Brig o' Feugh and into the Culter Burn. The Abbot's tower was demolished and the abbot himself ended up perched on a cole of hay.

July, that fifteenth dismal day,
This fearful spate began,

67

> And forty days and forty nights
> Rains fell, and torrents ran.

The moral of the story was simple – 'Beware of deep potations of grog and stout and ale'. But Davidson also said that a lesson should be learned from 'the churlish Abbot's fate'. Never refuse help to a neighbour in trouble, he said, or call him bad names if he now and then imbibes an extra glass of grog.

David Grant's classic 'Muckle Spate of Twenty-nine', written more than twenty years after Davidson's poem, carried echoes of 'The Legend of St Swithin', yet the St Swithin verse never achieved the lasting recognition that Grant's work did. Perhaps it was because the literary bookseller was a modest man, who 'loved anonymity and shrank from fame'.

When I went up St Swithin Street and crossed over to Fountainhall, I glanced up at the Queen, wondering if *she* had heard 'The Legend of St Swithin', with its mention of the River Dee and the Royal woods at Ballochbuie. After all, it was no secret that Victoria was fond of her grog. Up there, on her granite plinth, I could have sworn that I saw a smile on her lips.

Part II
Behind the Headlines

CHAPTER SEVEN

The Paper Chase

As I cam doon the Gallowgate
    An' through the Narrow Wynd,
Four and twenty weavers
    Were hanging on a twine,
The tow gaed a jerk
    And the weavers gaed a girn,
'O! lat me doon
    And I'll never steal anither pirn'.

Coming over the Gallowgate, I was thinking about the four and twenty weavers who were strung up on a 'twine' for pirn-stealing. I was thinking, too, of how this had once been an elegant street – the first *fashionable* street in Aberdeen, it was said, but then it had fallen on bad times and had become a disreputable slum, pitted with unsavoury closes. Today, the slums have gone, and in their place there is a dreary, soulless thoroughfare with high-rise flats that look down on an endless stream of traffic churning round the Mounthooly roundabout. They have something else to girn about now.

Up on top of the hill the flailing arms of the old windmill once whirled and clanked and beat time to a more leisurely way of life, but, like the gallows that gave the street its name, it has also vanished. So, too, has the soap factory – 'Soapy' Ogston's – along with the closes and courts that linked the Gallowgate with Lochside. One of the closes was M'Kay's Court, which was also known as the Candle Close. There is still a Candle Close today at No. 123 (the original was at No. 80), but it has little in common with the narrow, shabby lane that ran through Soapy's property eighty years ago. Nevertheless, the old close was home to Gallowgate folk and to keep it they were prepared to challenge the might of the Ogston empire.

Soapy wanted the Candle Close blocked off for an extension to his factory, ignoring the fact that it was an old right of way. When the matter came before the Town Council's streets and roads committee in November, 1917, its members were split on the proposal. There was talk about protecting rights-of-way and upholding 'the liberty of the people', but one member pointed out the lane was an eyesore and often in a filthy condition. Despite that, a census had shown that between 800 and 971 people used the close every day. At a public meeting in the Central Hall, Upperkirkgate, the chairman, George Gellie, said that the lane was important to working people who had a limited time to go for their meals, and another member thought that a substitute lane should be opened up for the sake of the children. Traffic in St Paul Street, he said, was dangerous.

The saga of the Can'le Closie rumbled on into 1918. One letter-writer to the *Aberdeen Free Press,* signing himself A.O. (Ancient o' Day), recalled that this wasn't the first Battle of the Closes. Some thirty-five years earlier, Alexander's Court had been closed and swallowed up by Ogston and Tennants. This old right-of-way had also run from the Gallowgate to Lochside, south of Innes Street. People living in the neighourhood had objected to its closure and decided to physically resist it. The first thing they did was put up barricades.

'The barricades erected in the lane were repeatedly destroyed', went 'A.O'.s' letter. 'The erection and breaking down continued for some time, but one evening the local patriots got a surprise when a flood from several hosepipes assailed them from over the walls of the soap works. Even this spate was combated for a time, but ultimately the cold-water cure was effectual and the public were literally sweeled out of their own property by a deluge from their own Invercannie!'*

When the 'battle' was over, a spectator was heard to remark that if Soapy Ogston's soap had been added to the water a litle benefit might have accrued to the 'great unwashed' engaged in the conflict.

The *Free Press* letter-writer, referring to a payment of £250 to be paid to the Council as compensation for a sewer, said that a Henry Gray had paid £100 to the Town Council for 'shutting up the dirty, narrow, useless Red Lion Court running between Broad Street and the Guestrow'. He also pointed out that when a pavement at Union Street and Alford Place had been repaired the Town Council had to pay £70 for a piece of ground that could have been covered 'by a large-sized tablecloth'.

'There is', wrote A.O., 'a Naboth's vineyard atmosphere about attacks on rights-of-way'. Naboth was a figure from the Old Testament, who was murdered by King Ahab at the instigation of his wife Jezebel for refusing to sell his vineyard. A.O. saw Lord Provost James Taggart as the King Ahab of the Gallowgate row, with 'Soapy' taking the role of Jezebel. He accused the Provost of summarily disposing of the matter without adequate discussion. It was, he said, an assault against a lane that for two generations had been known as the Candle Close, and which had been a direct path to the old Loch Side from the time the Gallowgate had been built. He pleaded with the Lord Provost to make the interests of the community his first consideration.

---

* The town's waterworks at Banchory.

Today there is not only a Can'le Closie, but also a Candlemaker's Court, off Loch Street, where there is a modern housing complex. The original Candlemaker's Close was at 46 Gallowgate. William Milne, a painter and glazier, lived nearby at Milne's Court, No. 60 Gallowgate, in the early nineteenth century. He made a name for himself by keeping a daily diary of the weather and by recording his own domestic transactions for every day of the year 1827.

Milne had a shop in the Guestrow near Provost Skene's House, better known then as Cumberland House or Cumberland Lodgings. The Guestrow was a busy place in those days, with a remarkable variety of businesses . . . bakers, tailors, dentists, musical instrument makers, slaters, wrights, boarding-house keepers and a lot more besides. By the early twentieth century, however, things had changed for the worse in a street that had housed not only Provost George Skene but the notorious Duke of Cumberland on his way to Culloden. For instance, the Red Lion Court, which ran between Broad Street and the Guestrow, was described as 'dirty, narrow and useless'. As G. M. Fraser put it delicately in his *Historical Aberdeen* in 1905, the Guestrow was 'not now a desired residential quarter'.

Yet Fraser saw beyond the dirt and dereliction. He thought that the Guestrow was 'not unpicturesque'. 'One may thread the back courts of its more interesting buildings with something of wonder', he wrote. In the grubby Red Lion Court he would have seen the last houses in the city with overhanging wooden gables. Neighbours in that squalid little street could reach across the court from their upstairs windows and shake hands with each other.

Fraser hoped that in time the authorities would 'find it possible to make way for larger masses of sunlight finding their way to many places that are now neither wholesome nor historic'. He could never have known that 'masses of sunlight' would one day shine on a Guestrow wasteland cleared of its buildings. There was nothing left to wonder at. The unwholesome houses had gone and the only historic building left was Provost Skene's House, which in time would itself be shut off from the sunlight, trapped inside the walls of an uninspiring municipal office block.

Almost directly across from Cumberland House is Queen Street, which linked the Broadgate and the Gallowgate with King Street, via what was known as the Back Causeway of North Street, now West North Street. That exit has long since been closed to traffic, so that now motorists have to find other devious routes to King Street. Some might think that a blessing, for King Street has had its critics over the years. Principal Sir William Geddes, who thought that the Gallowgate could be made as romantic and picturesque as Edinburgh's High Street, had nothing good to say about King Street. 'Dung carts and sewage, a poorhouse, a churchyard – with a hideous barrack and powder magazine – these form some of the attractions planted by way of adornment to the road', he wrote. More recently, Alex Keith, in his *A Thousand Years of Aberdeen*, put it more succinctly. 'King Street', he declared, 'is one of the dullest thoroughfares in the town'. It was a judgement that still stands.

King Street may have been dull, Queen Street certainly was not. It was described as a 'genteel' street, partly because of its literary associations. It was in this corner of the city, in an area roughly bounded by Queen Street, Broad Street, and Long Acre (formerly Long Acre Street), that a torrent of newspapers and periodicals poured out in the late eighteenth and early nineteenth centuries. One was the *Aberdeen Review*, founded in 1843 by John Mitchell, a crippled souter-poet who ran a bookseller's shop in Queen Street. Both the *Review* and its proprietor had short lives. Mitchell died in 1845 at the age of thirty-eight.

Farther up Queen Street was the office of the *Aberdeen Herald*, a building with a wide ornamental doorway and the type of architectural character that gave the street its 'genteel' appearance. Its sub-editor was another poet, William Forsyth, who later left it and went round the corner to Broad Street to become editor of the *Aberdeen Journal* for the next thirty years, standing down when the paper became a daily in 1877. When Forsyth was editing the *Journal* he often went to a Guestrow howff in the evening to discuss the next day's editorials with James Adam, the *Herald* editor. The *Herald*, which become a powerful campaigning paper under Adam's editorship, took over from the *Aberdeen Chronicle*, which gave its name to a street off Queen Street – Chronicle Street, later Chronicle Lane.

Meanwhile, over in Long Acre the printers were busy turning out periodicals with titillating titles that belonged more to the 'tabloid' twentieth century than to the nineteenth, among them the *Aberdeen Pirate*, the *Shaver*, the *Mirror* and the *Quizzing Glass*. They were following a trend set in 1832 when a Guestrow publisher, Robert Cobban, produced Aberdeen's first so-called 'comic' paper, the *Squib*. Cobban followed this up with a virulent monthly, the *Aberdeen Independent*. More than thirty 'comic' papers were produced during the thirties and almost the same number in the eighties.

For the most part, they traded in gossip and scandal, yet some of the city's most respected writers were among their contributors. One was John Ramsay, poet, raconteur and wit, who taught at Robert Gordon's Hospital before becoming a leader writer for the *Aberdeen Journal*. Ramsay and his contemporaries met regularly at Susie Affleck's (presumably a drinking howff) to enjoy life with 'the zest which youth, sound teeth and a good digestion gave them'.

Ramsay was often 'cock of the company'. From their meetings came 'a mass of glorious reading' which ultimately found its way into the pages of the *Shaver*, the *Quizzing Glass*, the *Pirate* and other periodicals. Much of it deserved to perish, but some was said to be 'good and pure' and would live on when the publications through which it first saw light were 'utterly forgotten'.

Today, these curious publications *are* forgotten, but so, too, is the 'good and pure' work which Ramsay contributed to the less scandalous papers. Perhaps the most important mark he made as a writer was in his editorials for the *Aberdeen Journal*. His leaders for the *Journal* were said to have a vigour and literary finish not common in a provincial paper. This son of a London ship-master always spoke in his 'native Doric' – his mother came from Blairdaff. He was an expert campanologist and often practised on the bells of St Nicholas Church. They were ringing when he died in June, 1870. When he heard them he whispered: 'These bells are not right placed.'

Broad Street wasn't always the home of the *Aberdeen Journal*, or *Aberdeen's Journal*, as it was originally called. It started life in a Castle Street building which had once been the printing house of Edward Raban, Aberdeen's first printer, and towards the end of the eighteenth century it moved to an old silk-mill behind the Town House. In 1813 it flitted again to Adelphi Court, finally coming to a rest in the office of the defunct *Northern Daily News* in Broad Street. The *Northern News* was Aberdeen's first evening paper. It was incorporated with the *Evening Express* in 1893, boosting the *Express's* circulation to 10,000.

There was another newspaper in Broad Street long before the *Journal* arrived there. This was the *Aberdeen Banner,* edited by David Masson, and it was one of a number of newspapers that gave the *Journal* a run for its money in the 1840s. In the *Aberdeen Directory* for 1848–49 ninety-two houses are shown in Broad Street. There were booksellers and tailors, haircutters and corkcutters, shoemakers and watchmakers, grocers and vintners. The *Banner's* office was listed at No. 64 Broad Street.

The folk of Broad Street must have had a sweet tooth in the old days, for a number of confectioners appear in the Directory. William Shepherd is entered as a *late* confectioner at No. 40, where there were six tenants, while a confectioner called George Sharp operated from No. 64 – the building where the *Aberdeen Banner* had its office. A Mrs Kerr had a coffee room in the same building. Farther down Broad Street a couple called B. and W. M'Killiam had a confectionery shop at No. 52.

M'Killiam is an unusual name. I had come upon it before and it niggled in my mind for a long time; then I remembered where I had first seen it.

This was in an old photograph of the *Aberdeen Journal* office in Broad Street as it was in the days when papers were delivered by pony and trap. Three traps could be seen in the picture, loaded up with bundles of *Evening Expresses*, ready to go. The office was flanked on one side by a wholesale warehouse and on the other by a shop with a partly-obscured sign. It read 'B & W. McKilliam'. Upstairs was a window carrying a notice, 'Coffee Room'. So here, at the other end of Broad Street, another newspaper office had a confectioner and a coffee room on its doorstep.

Broad Street. To the right of the *Evening Express* sign is the office where the author worked as an office boy. It was originally a sweetie shop.

But the name McKilliam brought back other memories for me. Sixty years ago I walked through the door of that old sweetie shop to begin work as an office boy with Aberdeen Journals. Long before that the shop had been taken over by the newspaper and turned into a public office. People placed their classified 'ads' and paid their bills there and at the end of a counter which ran the length of the room I had a small desk. One of my duties was to lick stamps for the outgoing mail. There was no new technology in the shape of wet rollers in those days, so I literally licked my way into my new job.

I must have been a competent stamp-licker, for I was promoted upstairs to the sub-editors' room, away from the commercial workings of the newspaper. In the 'subs' I had my first taste of real newspaper life, or, at any rate, the editorial side of it. People talked mysteriously about editions and deadlines, 'splash' headlines and 'stoppers', and I scuttled backwards and forwards to the caseroom (composing room) with the latest stories from the newsroom. I had become a 'copy' boy. Somewhere under the creaking old building I could hear the muffled roar of the printing presses as the papers 'went to bed'. I knew then that this was where my future lay, that I had joined the paper chase. But my ambitions at that time were limited – I just wanted to be part of the newspaper scene. There was no crystal ball to tell me that one day I would be editor of the *Evening Express*, a job I was to hold for twenty-two years.

The McKilliams were bakers as well as confectioners. Weddings and other functions were held in a small hall attached to the bakery. The sound of music and merry-making was often heard by sub-editors on the other side of the wall dividing the bakery from the newspaper office, but that came to an end when the *Journal* decided to expand and bought the premises. A curious hotch-potch of old buildings had occupied the site of the Northern Daily News . . . old tenements, a dance hall, the bakery, a chemist's shop and an undertaker's parlour. The coffins were still there when the *Aberdeen Journal* moved in.

Two centuries of newspaper history were made in that cramped old office, with its maze of gloomy corridors, its closes, wandering stairways and smoke-filled rooms. When I became the subs' boy I got to know the first-floor corridor well. The Kemsleys were sometimes spotted flitting wraith-like along it, keeping an eye on their property. The Marchioness of Huntly, daughter of Lord Kemsley, was seen but seldom heard; not, at any rate, by the staff. She was Pamela Berry, who married the Marquis of Huntly. There was a story told about how she saw a photograph of a huge Aberdeen-Angus bull in the 'P&J' and wanted it 'doctored'. Oswald Berry was sent up from London to learn the ropes, but he, too, was remote from the common herd. I had to run to a tobacconist's shop in Union Street to get Three Castle cigarettes for him.

The bulky figure of Alexander Keith – 'A.K.' – once tramped along that corridor. He was leader writer and assistant editor of the *Journal*, but he resigned when William Veitch got the job he thought should have been his – editor-in-chief. Veitch succeeded Sir William Maxwell in 1927, became managing director and editor-in-chief, and retired in 1957. He had his office on the first floor, with an access door from the sub-editors' room, and in the days before war broke out one of my duties as subs' boy was to creep into his room two or three times a day and hang up the latest news bills on two hooks near his window.

When I was demobbed from the RAF after the war, I went back to to D.C. Thomson, where I had been a trainee reporter, and started work in the Aberdeen office of the *People's Journal'* for a salary of £5 a week. I moved quickly up to Broad Street, coaxed by the offer of another £2, and found myself back on the first floor – a reporter on the old *Weekly Journal*, edited by Cuthbert Graham. There were new faces on the first-floor in those post-war years. At the end of the corridor was the *Press and Journal* editor's room, occupied successively by James M. Chalmers (1944–1950), George Ley Smith (1950–1956), Kenneth Peters (1956–1960), and James C. Grant (1960–1975). Ken

Bob Smith, then Editor of the *Evening Express*, breaks the metal plate which symbolised the end of the Broad Street era. Jimmy Grant (left), Editor of the *Press and Journal*, also took part in this tradition.

Peters, who edited the *Evening Express* from 1953 to 1956, became managing director in 1960.

Another first-floor occupant was Eddie Balloch, who wrote a highly-controversial 'Jack Adrian' column. He was assistant to William Veitch and was expected to take over his job, but some difference of opinion put an end to that. Many years later I wrote a column under the name of Rex Baird. It had a Jack Adrian flavour about it and frequently landed me in hot water. Another familiar Broad Street figure at that time was George Fraser, who was editor of the *Evening Express* from 1944 to 1953. He joined the *Daily Journal* in 1917, beginning a career that was to last through nine decades, making him Britain's oldest working journalist.

The Broad Street saga came to an end when Aberdeen Journals Ltd took the decision to move to new premises at Mastrick in 1970. It was a shift that

A coffin carrying the last papers to be printed in Broad Street are ceremoniously carried from the building before the move to Mastrick.

many people, particularly the editorial staff, resented. It was removing them from familiar, friendly surroundings, cramped and cluttered though they were, and putting them into a factory. That's what some people called it; there was no journalistic ambience in this alien corner of the town. It was also taking them away from the city centre, from the Town House and the police and the courts, from the news that had always been on their doorstep. They were remembering the days when Broad Street was crammed on a Saturday afternoon with Dons' fans waiting for the *Green Final* to hit the streets. They were recalling, too, how the office had been beseiged by news-hungry readers during the sensational Garvie trial, and they were thinking of John Baird's City Bar in the Netherkirkgate, which had been their drinking howff for as long as they could remember.

The curtain came down on Saturday, 14 November, 1970. That was when the sports edition of the *Evening Express* was printed – the last *Green Final* to roll off the presses in Broad Street. When the machines fell silent the metal plate of the front page was taken from the rollers and placed in a makeshift coffin, then carried ceremoniously to the despatch room, where Jimmy Grant, the 'P&J' editor, and myself were given hammers to break it up in traditional fashion. Then we adjourned to the City Bar to celebrate – or to mourn the passing of an era.

Bob Smith with the Queen Mother during her visit to the new Aberdeen Journals office at the Lang Stracht. Behind is Jimmy Grant, Editor of the *Press and Journal*.

The coffin that was borne to the despatch room on that November day had more than a metal plate in it, for we were burying a way of life, scrapping old practices, abandoning outworn ideas, moving on in the newspaper game to the new techniques and new challenges that lay ahead in the last years of the twentieth century. The ghosts of the past were with us then. They are still with us today, for history often repeats itself. Past and present are irretrievably linked, for controversies that hit the headlines in the 20th century were often echoes of events that took place in the 19th century, as the following chapters show. Lord Provost Rust said that the pages of the city's history carried lessons for the future. To know them you have to look behind the headlines – into the 'hidden city' of this book.

CHAPTER EIGHT

Between the Covers

Aberdonians have always had an innate fondness for journalism. Alexander Keith, one-time assistant editor of the old *Aberdeen Journal.* and himself a distinguished journalist, once said that this was shown very early in the modern history of the Fourth Estate*. The literature of the North-east is peppered with the names of well-known journalists who wrote about their own city, men like Alex Keith himself, with his *Thousand Years of Aberdeen*, or Cuthbert Graham and his *Portrait of Aberdeen and Deeside*, or Robert Anderson, chief sub-editor of the *Free Press* and editor of the *Journal*, who wrote *Aberdeen in Bygone Days*. There were many more.

This is the story of two reporters who made good in the newspaper business . . . and of how, in their different ways, they left a unique picture of life in the 'hidden city' in the second half of the nineteenth century and in the early years of the twentieth.

George Milne Fraser was in his early twenties when he decided he wanted to become a newspaper reporter. It seemed a curious ambition for a young man who had been brought up on a farm and trained as a stonecutter with an Aberdeen firm of monumental masons. But fate plays strange tricks. Fraser achieved his ambition – by losing an eye in an accident at work.

No longer able to carry on his work in the granite trade, he went to William Alexander, Editor of the *Free Press,* and asked him for a job. That was in 1887, sixteen years after Alexander had written his Doric classic, *Johnny Gibb of Gushetneuk*, and young Fraser, a shy country loon, must have been overawed by the great man. Alexander set him a task that was to test his shyness. He was sent to a hall in Blackfriars Street and told to write an account of a lecture on the subject of the American poet Ralph Waldo Emerson.

Fraser, the farm lad from Methlick, knew little about Emerson. He knew even less about reporting and he was too shy to sit and take notes under the gaze of the public. The words were stored in his mind, but he couldn't pluck up enough courage to go back to the *Free Press* office and put them together. Instead, he wrote his report in the street, outside a tobacconist's shop in Hadden Street, scribbling his first newspaper story by the light from a gas lamp inside the shop window.

---

*The Press

The result was that Alexander offered him a job. He never knew how much, if at all, the decision was influenced by the fact that Alexander's brother, Henry, who was to succeed him as editor, had also lost an eye. At any rate, both brothers gave him encouragement and understanding and Fraser quickly showed that he had a way with words. In the next thirteen years he won a reputation as a competent, accurate reporter. It was the first stage in a career that was to earn him an important niche in the local literary scene – and to launch him into a new career in the book world.

George Fraser was born on 31 October, 1862, at the farm of Haddo at Methlick. His father, Joseph Fraser, was a farm servant, his grandfather a blacksmith in the village of Gamrie, and his mother Mary Taylore, the daughter of a Strichen farm worker. George was the fourth of a family of twelve.

In the late 1860s the Fraser family moved to Aberdeen so that Joseph Fraser could get work in the booming granite industry. They moved to a house in Minister Lane, where many years later Davie Duncan was brought up (see Chapter Two). Davie was to tell in his book *Tenements and Sentiments* how as a school pupil he was taken to hear G.M. Fraser lecture on the history of Aberdeen and was inspired to write, just as Fraser himself had been inspired by Dr William Alexander.

George was largely self-educated. Two of his younger brothers, Joe and Alex, also became apprentice stonecutters. When George began work as a reporter he wrote for both the *Free Press* and its sister paper, the *Evening Gazette*. His job opened new doors for him. He met people from all walks of life, among them industrialists, politicians, educationists and churchmen. He discovered a taste for local history. He learned about his adopted city, its streets, its buildings, its characters. He was storing away information that would one day be used in the books that he wrote.

Fraser was destined for an editor's chair, but in 1899 he took a decision that changed his life. He applied for the vacant post of Aberdeen City Librarian. Up to that time it had been held by A.W. Robertson, Aberdeen's first librarian, who in 1893 had issued a *Handlist of Bibliography of the Shires of Aberdeen, Banff and Kincardine*. Robertson was retiring at the early age of fifty-two to give time to his studies. When the post was advertised in the local press and in leading national literary journals, there were thirty-nine applications. Twenty-five of the applicants were experienced librarians.

A short leet of six was drawn up – and on it was the name of George Milne Fraser, journalist. You could almost *feel* the sense of shock that went through the ranks of the local intelligentsia . . . a newspaperman, a reporter, a hack, applying for the Librarian's post! It was unthinkable. Letters of complaint, carrying pseudonyms like 'Bibliophile No. 2', and 'Literary Scavenger', began to flow into the offices of the *Evening Express* and the *Aberdeen Journal*, reaching their peak a few days before the decision was taken.

Most of the complaints were about George Fraser's lack of experience. 'No man with a particle of honour or business aptitude would aspire to a situation, the duties of which he was entirely ignorant of', wrote 'One Who Knows'. 'Or, if he did apply it would afford the best proof of his unfitness for the appointment.' The writer had a sting in the tail – 'The claims of the journalist are strongly supported by the Labour clique', he wrote. This brought a quick reply from 'Anti Job', who said that if there was 'any little dodgery' it should be exposed.

'A terror seems to exist in the minds of not a few citizens that the appointment is likely to fall to a layman and not a professional', wrote 'Straight', and went on to say that a good, level-headed businessman would make the best librarian to Aberdeen, 'even although he had never been inside a librarian's "sanctum sanctorum" before'.

The Library Committee met on Saturday, 30 December, 1899, to cast their votes. Councillor Johnston referred to letters and articles in the newspapers about the appointment. 'Some of the letters were of a somewhat scurrilous nature', he said. Despite that, it turned out that George Fraser had influential supporters. He supplied the committee with seventeen testimonials from lawyers, professors and clergymen. He was appointed by thirteen votes to seven.

Printer's ink still ran through George Fraser's veins during his time as Aberdeen's Librarian. He contributed to countless newspapers and periodicals under the initials 'G.M.F'. and some of these articles were included in the books that he wrote. His first book, *The Green and its Story,* was published in 1904, and after that came *Historical Aberdeen.* There were others, including *The Old Deeside Road.* In the summer of 1909 he wrote a series of articles on street names for the *Aberdeen Evening Gazette,* and these formed the basis of a book that is still selling today – *Aberdeen Street Names.* It introduced readers to the mysteries of such seedy back alleys as the 'Shelly' Close, the Vennel (the worst slum in Aberdeen) and the 'Bool' Road, and it told them how streets like Correction Wynd and the Guestrow got their names.

It was reprinted in 1986 with a supplement and foreword written by Moira Henderson. Moira, who formerly worked in the local reference department of the library, described Fraser as small, spare and bespectacled, usually dressed in a grey suit, white shirt and winged collar, but donning plus-fours when he went on outings with the Deeside Field Club. 'His name', she wrote in an introduction to *Aberdeen Street Names*, 'was known all over the North-east and certainly the audiences at the Beach Pavilion were in no doubt as to his identity when they shouted his name in a chorus to one of Harry Gordon's most popular songs.'

Aberdeen Library's Local Collection was 'his finest memorial'. G.M. Fraser was responsible for acquiring much of its valuable stock. Yet, oddly enough, in a cabinet in the local reference department there is a mass of material collected by Fraser that few people have seen or even know about . . . a 'hidden' treasure-chest of information about the city and its people. There are seventy volumes of what are known as Fraser's Notebooks. Between their black covers are notes and cuttings on almost every subject under the sun – the letting of the New Inn (6 December, 1815), a general meeting of the Shiprow Society (November, 1815), a paragraph about contractors who were 'wanted to pave the carriage way of Young Street, with Quarry Chips (May, 1827), and so on.

Here and there are copies of photographs of such vastly assorted subjects as the Prop of Ythsie at Haddo, a painting by William Dyce, and Queen Victoria receiving the Keys of the City at Love Lane, King Street, on her visit to Aberdeen in 1857. There are advertisements for pawnbrokers (advances from £5 to £5,000) and notes on Aberdeen's old clockmakers. A whole volume is given over to Aberdeen's boundary stones:

4 June 1921 – Examined No. 1 stone in cellar at 81 Hardgate. Found it (& adjoining stone marker 'C.R'.) precisely as described in Robert Anderson's pamphlet 'The Riding of the Marches' 1889, P114. Mr Harper, of the shop No. 79. who took me down to the cellar, mentioned that official inspections by the Town Council take place every now and again – eight or ten carriages, he said (which seemed rather an astonishing number).

Fraser was a literary magpie, peck-pecking at every glittering prize that came his way, storing it away for future reference. His notebooks throw up titbits of information that might never have been known to future generations; for instance, the fact that St Machar Drive was almost given the name 'Ave Maria Drive'. The naming of a new road from Woodside to Old Aberdeen was argued over in the letter columns of the *Free Press*, the *Evening Express* and the *Journal*. The name Ave Maria Drive was suggested by a *Free Press* reader signing himself 'Woodside'. He said that 'the road abuts at a point where once stood the statue on the gateway bearing the Latin legend *Hac ne vade via, nisi dixeris Ave Maria*. It fell by the wayside when it was pointed out that it was a 'euphonious word laying itself open to grotesque pronounciation'. Cathedral Drive, Elphinstone Drive, Aulton Drive, Chanonry Drive all came into the reckoning, but in the end the choice was St Machar Drive.

Then there was Babbie Law, who achieved a measure of immortality when her name was used to mark out the length of Union Street – 'Fae the Duke tae Babbie Law'. But who *was* Babbie Law? Well, in April, 1921, someone signing himself 'C.S'. wrote to the *Press and Journal* announcing proudly, 'I had the pleasure of knowing Babie Law and her sister, Ellen, who kept a grocer's shop at Wellington Place, close by Holburn Church. A sign above the door bore the legend, 'B. Law, late with John Dunn. Licensed to sell tea, tobacco and spirits.

'Babie sold a good dram, and, in common with most grocers of the day, was ready to give a friend what he required behind the shelter of the treacle cask, or if he were a special friend, seated in comfort in her private sanctum. The law began to be more vigorously enforced and this had to cease. It is fifty years since Babie's door was finally closed, and to very few there remains the memory of a very interesting and kindly personality.'

Many of the entries in the notebooks were pencilled in and are hard to read. This is made more even more difficult by Fraser's occasional use of Pitman's shorthand – a legacy from his reporting days. He would start a sentence and switch to shorthand in the middle of it, as he did when copying this line about the Market Cross, written in 1821:

> We understand there is (some prospect of the) interior of the Cross, now rebuilding (being fitted up as the) Post Office for this city.

Another piece of long-running correspondence revolved around a reader's query about the phrase 'Hale Rick-ma-Tick'. One letter was from G. M. Fraser himself. He thought it was 'a degraded form of the expression 'The whole a-rith-me-tic (arithmetic)', meaning the total, the whole thing. Another reader, James Cassie, agreed with him and quoted a verse he had heard:

> Th' warl' is noo turn't upside doon,
> Tho' folk a'buff ower quick;
> As sure's a'm here a'm wearit' wi'
> Th' hale rick-ma-tick.

W. Clark Mitchell, from Schoolhill, said it came from a song sung in the Alhambra Theatre in Market Street. Two of the lines went:

> It's nae the warl we live in, but the folk
> that mak's me sick,
> A' help my bob, I'm scunnered wi' the
> hale-rick-ma-tick.

Poems, pictures, tales of the old coaching days (the Defiance, the Queen of Beauty, the New Times), discussion on the Aberdeen dialect, paragraphs about the selling of the Wallace Nook and Fountainhall House, a comment about vaccination ('apathy in the lower classes'), a note about the Aberdeenshire Canal fly boats . . . they pack the pages of Fraser's Notebooks, a valuable record of bygone days on the one hand, a gold mine of trivia on the other. In the new millenium, some researcher will pore over these little black books and marvel at them – the hale rick-ma-tick. George Milne Fraser, the man who put them together, died on 7 June, 1938, at the age of seventy-five.

A poem in one of Fraser's notebooks carried the lines:

'I mind mysel' on Carnie fine,
wi' his rich, mirth-provoking line'.

This was William Carnie, poet, musician, sub-editor – and reporter. He was born in the Green in 1824 and when he left school he was sent as an apprentice to an engraver in the Netherkirkgate. But his two great loves were music and writing, and this was where his career lay. He worked on the *North of Scotland Gazette* before going to the *Aberdeen Herald* in 1852. He was employed as a sub-editor and reporter and became a music critic of note, as well as a drama critic. In 1854 he brought together a choir of 1,000 voices.

Queen Victoria, opening the Cairnton water scheme at Banchory in October, 1866, made a remark about 'my neighbours of Aberdeen'. When her statue was unveiled at St Nicholas Street in 1893, the Cairnton ceremony was recalled in a poem read by William Cairnie at 'an important public assemblage of citizens' in the Grand Hotel to celebrate the raising of the statue:

'Twas a merry morn at Cairnton, a festive day I trow,
When there our Queen, in graceful speech,
   made Dee's bright water flow,
The cheers rang through the woods around,
   as 'mid that autumn scene
Sir Alexander bowed his best for -
      'My neighbours of Aberdeen'.

That mawkish poem, full of sentimental phrases about 'braif old Bon-Accord', glowing with 'pomp and glee', marvelling at 'yon sculptured form' of the Royal statue, was scarcely the 'mirth-provoking' lines for which Carnie was remembered – rich Doric poems like 'Hirpletillim', about an out-of-the-way spot at Rubislaw Den, and his 'Toon Hoose' sketch of Saunders Munro, who looked after the town's cash:

Saunders keeps the Toon Cash; looks weel aifter the till,
And o' ilk Deputation wad keep doon the bill:
Yet at hame, for the honour of braif Bon-Accord,
He wide slackens the purse strings o' Council or Board.

William Carnie's most notable work came from his years as a reporter. His three volumes of *Reporting Reminiscences* were said to be an eye-witness account of the town during the second half of the nineteenth century. In a preface to the first volume, published in 1902, he said it was the result of 'friendly pressure from indulgent fellow citizens to put on record in homely running commentary form some personal experiences of Aberdeen folk and doings during the early years of my newspaper life'. The second volume came in 1904 and the third in 1906, two years before he died.

Poets and politicians, clowns and campanologists (Aberdeen had a Campanologian Band in the mid-18th century) Provosts and philosophers, admirals and actors, mechanics and murderers . . . they marched through the pages of Carnie's *Reminiscences* in an endless, ghostly parade. Deacon Alexander Robb – tailor, poet, and, said Carnie, 'a lichtsome companion' – was there, reciting his poetry, recalling 'simmer days' when it was roasting hot and they ran to the Provost's Pot to 'get a glorious dook':

> Afore our sarks gaed ower our head
> Ye'll a' remember how
> We riped our pooches aye for bread
> To be a chiverin" chow.*

Carnie wrote at length about the theatrical life of the city, and particularly about places of entertainment like Mrs Liffen's Hall at the Adelphi Hotel, where they held a series of evening concerts under the chairmanship of Sam Cowell, who was said to be one of the best comic singers of the day. His *Villikins and his Dinah* ditties, said Carnie, 'caught on marvellously'. Another popular entertainer at Liffens was Little Barlow, 'a dainty warbler and master of the banjo'. His singing, with imitation accompaniment, about a bee buzzing around his instrument was 'almost perfect'.

But Carnie's reporting skills were seen at their best in his coverage of the big stories. In 1856, plans by two railway companies to open a railway line to Peterhead resulted in what he called 'one of the very fiercest, long-drawn-out contests ever experienced'. The reason – one of the proposed lines would run through the Links, the only public park in the city. When a House of Commons standing committee approved the plan, a public meeting was held in Castle Street under the chairmanship of the Lord Provost. 'A great crowd assembled', wrote Carnie. 'The proceedings became, more than once, quite uproarious, indeed dangerous, the vast multitude crushing in upon the table constituting the platform for the speakers till the poor uncared for reporters were within an inch of their lives, or rather deaths.

'Indeed, William Alexander proudly asserted that he saved his pencilling companions from broken legs by the happy device of inserting his stout artificial limb between two tables, upon one of which we were sitting at work! For the purpose of voting by show of hands two placards bearing in large type "Preserve the Links" and "Give up the Links" were displayed. A hundred hands strove to get at the latter and it was speedily trampled under foot.'

The Battle of the Links moved from the Castlegate to the columns of the local newspapers and in the end the Commons standing committee reversed its decision and threw out the plan. The Links were saved!

---

*riped – searched. chow – mouthful

Carnie's *Reminiscences* moved 'from the stage and footlights to the heath-clad hills and howes of Crathie' – to 1855 when the Braemar gathering was held at Braemar Castle. Carnie's account started with the arrival of 'the Forbes men', who had 'tramped from their trysting place, Clachan of Tornaish, Corgarff, across country from Strathdon and are encamped at Tynabaigh, exactly opposite Balmoral Castle, where Her Majesty, the Prince Consort with the Royal children, and the Court are still in residence. Hearty Highland revelry rings forth from the pitched tents.'

Carnie described how a cry went up, 'The Prince is coming!' The Forbes men hurried into a 'soldier-like reception order'. Then, looking down the river, they could see Prince Albert mounted on a pony fording the Dee with his attendants to visit the camp. Hospitality flowed freely – the Prince moved among the tents and soon after that a messenger arrived with mutton and whisky for the men and wine for the officers – a gift from the Queen. Next day, Victoria visited the camp and in the evening there were 'private rejoicings' at Invercauld House. Carnie was there with a number of other reporters. 'Our note-taking duty accomplished', he wrote, 'we took a walk down to the comfortable inn at Inver and enjoyed ourselves.'

The Forbes march from Strathdon to Braemar was renacted a few years ago when the men of Lonach tramped across the hills to the Braemar Gathering. There was no visit to their encampment by the Queen – and no fording the Dee by the present Queen's Consort. The part played by the Royal Family in today's Gathering seems tame by comparison with that colourful scene a century and a half ago.

CHAPTER NINE

The Auld Express

A few years ago I was sent a birthday card which carried the message: '1923 was a Special Year'. It was the year I was born. I learned from the card that my birthday was shared by Franco Zefferelli, Henry Kissinger, Charlton Heston, and that luvvie of stage and screen, 'Dickie' Attenborough. It also told me that 1923 was the year in which Stanley Baldwin became Prime Minister, the French fashion queen Gabrielle 'Coco' Chanel launched a new perfume, and Suzanne Lenglen won the Wimbledon Ladies' Singles for the fifth successive year.

Among the 1923 events listed on the card were some which were to touch or affect my life in the years to come . . . the Nazi party held its first rally in Munich, Adolf Hitler staged a coup attempt, and the Duke of York married Lady Elizabeth Bowes Lyon – the future Queen Mum, whose path I was to cross many times during my newspaper years.

I remember looking back the files to find out what momentous events had happened in Aberdeen in the year of my birth. There were no meteors flashng through the sky, no great portents for the future. The only significant entry I could find was that hundreds of cats had died in the city. 'So widespread has been the feline mortality', reported the *Evening Express*, 'that in several districts of the city suspicions of a wholesale poisoning scheme have been aroused'. In the end, what the paper called the 'epidemic of death' was put down to cold weather.

Being a newspaperman, dates and anniversaries have always played a big part in my life. The headlines splashed across the front pages of Aberdeen's evening paper were milestones in my career . . . disasters, weddings, elections, moon landings, municipal rows, sea tragedies, they were the raw material which found its way on to endless miles of newsprint. But the pages and headlines that stayed in my mind over the years didn't always spring from day-to-day 'hard news'. For instance, one headline was written when my editorship was coming to an end. Set in bold black type – TWENTY NOT OUT – it dominated a 'mock' front page produced by my staff to mark my two decades in the Editor's chair (see Chapter Ten).

Three pictures ran above it. One, dated 1980, was taken when we celebrated what was said to be 'a great year for the 'E.E.' – the year when our daily average sale hit over 82,000 copies, which was no mean feat in a declining evening paper market. Seven years earlier, in 1973, we were toasting a different kind of success – the end of a campaign to raise money to buy home dialysis machines for kidney patients in Aberdeen and the North-east. We called it the Lifeline Appeal.

Lifeline was one of a number of charity campaigns I ran in the paper. I didn't know it then, but I was maintaining a tradition that went back more than a century to the time when the *Evening Express* raised over £1,000 for the relief of the unemployed, and to the Boer War, when a fund called 'Those Left Behind' raised nearly £5,000 for the widows and children of soldiers who had fallen in the war. There were many more appeals connected with gale disasters and shipwrecks.

Despite the fact that our forbears had happily dipped into their pockets for charity appeals, the hoary old myth of the mean Aberdonian still existed. I had the feeling that the Lifeline appeal demolished it once and for all. For fifteen months the money poured in . . . from whist drives, beetle drives, raffles, sponsored walks, fashion shows, coffee mornings. A prisoner in Craiginches donated a magnificent 18-inch long galleon made from matches and we offered it to the reader who could calculate to the nearest figure the number of matches used. The total was 13,975 – and the galleon went to a Portsoy salmon fisher.

Contributions came from as far away as the south of England and the island of Yell in Shetland. In April, 1973, we announced the final figure – £36,000. We had set out to buy a renal dialysis machine; we ended up with enough money to buy fourteen of them. I realised just how much they meant to kidney patients when I handed over the first machine to an Aberdeen man, Hugh McKay. His life was no longer ruled by visits to the hospital for dialysis treatment; now he was able to carry out this life-saving operation in his own home.

'It's a bit like a fairy story', wrote reporter Jennifer Simon. 'It doesn't seem real that from such humble beginings the appeal, like Topsy, just "growed and growed". Nine people have already had machines installed in their homes and they have no doubt about its reality.

'Looking back at last summer, the outstanding memory is one of armies of schoolchildren who besieged the *Evening Express* office at Mastrick to hand over the proceeds from jumble sales held during their holidays. Not a day went by without the ranks being formed up outside by a photographer to "tak' their photy" for Lifeline. Puzzled onlookers who asked what it was all about were told, "That's Bob Smith's kids!".'

Hundreds of people travelled on Lifeline excursion trains to Kyle of Lochalsh, and it was there that the final cheque for £36,000 was handed over to Dick Spain, chairman of the North-east Regional Hospital Board. One of the passengers on the train was Hugh McKay.

Hugh McKay was the first Aberdeen man to receive a kidney machine from the Lifeline Appeal. Here, Hugh and his wife are seen with the machine when it was installed in their home and handed over by Bob Smith, Editor of the *Express*.

In 1981, Lifeline was totally eclipsed by another appeal – Laser Line. It all began when Bill Crosby, then chairman of the Hospital Board, invited me to lunch to discuss the possibility of another appeal. Buff Hardie, of 'Scotland the What?', who worked with the hospital board, was also there. They wondered if I would be willing to launch a campaign for a body-scanner for the hospital. 'How much would that cost?' I asked. After a moment's hesitation, I got the answer – £280,000 – nearly ten times the amount raised for Lifeline.

I turned down the invitation. I doubted if that amount of money could be raised in a local newspaper appeal. What if it ground to a halt, I asked, what if there were no 'Bob's kids' at the door on a Monday morning. And if it did fail, how could I tell our readers that it was all off, finished, that we would never be able to make our target, that there would be no body scanner for the hospital. Failure would look bad for the paper, and bad for the hospital board. But in the end, against my better judgement, I said I would give it a try. Maybe it was the memory of those kids handing over their week-end cash that did it, or maybe it was the thought of the lives that could be saved by a new body scanner.

I should have had more faith in my fellow-Aberdonians. This time we climbed the heights in more ways than one. Blind Duncan Simpson, a friend of mine for many years, wanted to do a sponsored walk for the appeal – up Cairngorm! As a safety measure, I asked Malcolm Duckworth, leader of the Aberdeen Mountain Rescue team, if he would join us. He agreed, and turned up with the whole team. We pushed our way up, the Cairngorm hills spreading majestically all around us. We were going up over 4,000 feet, bagging a 'Munro', but more important than that we were giving a major boost to the Laser Line campaign.

I took a bottle of whisky with me to give the climbers a drink when we reached the top, and it turned out that my wife, Sheila, had also secretly taken a bottle with her because it was my birthday. Joan Elrick, a reporter with the paper, had baked a cake and Gordon Bisset, our photographer, himself an experienced climber, had made a birthday banner. It was the strangest birthday celebration I had ever had – no other birthday was ever likely to match it. We stood on the top of Cairngorm, the wind gusting across the summit, the banner unfurled – Happy Birthday! – and, crouching round the cake, sheltering from the wind, we lit the candles. Duncan, who ran a tape service for the blind, recorded the event, then we toasted Laser Line, drank the whisky, and made our way down the hill.

There were many other sponsored walks and money-raising events and on 7 July, 1981, the *Evening Express* carried another headline that was to linger in my memory for many years – YOU'VE DONE IT . . . THANKS A MILLION! 'With one almighty shove', wrote Joan Elrick, 'we've gone tearing past our £280,000 target to £288,000'. The money that pushed the appeal 'over the top' came from Gillian Macaulay, a former Scottish international swimmer, who swam 146 lengths of Hazlehead Pool to raise £480 for Laser Line. Gillian did her mammoth swim with her brother Ranald. For them it had a special significance, for it took place exactly a year after the death of their mother, Irene Fordyce. Irene and James Fordyce, both well-known Aberdeen swimmers, died within four months of each other from lung cancer. Both had been friends of my wife, who swam with them in their school days.

There was another poignant footnote to the Laser Line campaign. When it was all over, a small plaque commemorating the appeal was put up in the entrance hall of the Royal Infirmary. That day, a young boy was given a brain scan – the first patient to be put through the new body-scanning machine. Sadly, it showed that nothing could be done for him. I felt a sense of hopelessness when I was told this, but it was pointed out that even with this result the scanner had proved its worth. Without it, there would have been painful operations that would have come to nothing.

Another page that I remember very clearly was published in January, 1979. It carried the headline 'Congratulations on 100 years of the Evening Express'. Messages marking the paper's centenary came from all over the North and North-east, from the Queen, from the Dons, from lairds and lords; many from

Bill Crosby, chairman of the North-east Hospital Board, receives a Laser Line cheque from Bob Smith, Editor of the Evening Express. The money raised for a new body scanner totalled £288,000.

MPs whose names have vanished from the political scene, among them Russell Johnston, MP for Inverness, Russell Fairgrieve, MP for West Aberdeenshire, Ian Sproat, MP for South Aberdeen, and Douglas Henderson, MP for East Aberdeenshire. Hamish Watt, who was then MP for Banffshire, said that the paper was affectionately known in his North-east neuk simply as 'the 'Evening'. It was, he commented, 'part of the very fabric of our lives.'

That old warrior, Mike Mackie – Maitland Mackie, Lord-Lieutenant of Aberdeenshire – sent a message that might well have been his own motto – 'Don't feel old', he said, 'feel good'. John Smith, later Lord Kirkhill, who was Lord Provost when the oil boom hit the city, sent his good wishes.

Chief Constable Donald Henderson, of the Northern Constabulary, also sent his congratulations. I had come to know and respect him during the sensational Macrae mystery in Inverness. In 1976, Renee Macrae and her 3-year-old son Andrew disappeared from their home in Inverness. Her BMW was discovered blazing in a layby on the Perth to Inverness road and no trace has ever been found of them.

A year after her disappearance the *Evening Express* and the Northern Constabulary decided to co-operate on a major investigation into the case. The result was a three-part investigation followed by a 'final analysis' on the fourth

Blind Duncan Simpson on top of Cairngorm after taking part in a sponsored climb of the mountain in aid of the Laser Liune Appeal. With him is his son Kenneth.

day. The first two days of the investigation were based on researches by assistant news editor David Smith, Inverness chief reporter Jim Love and reporters Bruce McKain, Eric Crockart and Helen Lumsden. They featured appeals from the missing woman's husband and Chief Constable Henderson. A session in an Inverness hotel room was chaired by myself as editor. Six key figures to the mystery were brought together for the first time. It cast a fascinating light on what was known as the 'Macrae Mystery', but more than twenty years later it remains unsolved.

Andy Stewart added his name to the centenary well-wishers, saying it in verse from his home at Transcona, Banchory:

Lighting candles on top of Cairngorm – a birthday surprise for Bob Smith, Editor of the *Evening Times*.

A hunner years has been the stint,
Sin' first ye started up in print;
An' since the day ye did begin't
Ye've seen success –
Sae here's tae the neist five score you'll rin't,
The auld 'Express'.

The auld 'Express' was launched on Monday, 20 January, 1879. Its price –
one halfpenny. An anouncement about the new paper was carried in the
Aberdeen Journal, which described it as 'a first-class local newspaper with
telegraphic general and commercial news'. This testimonial from its sister

Blind Duncan Simpson with the mountain rescue members who climbed Cairngorm to raise money for the Laser Line Appeal.

paper got the *Express* off to a good start, for there was such a demand for the first issue that the printing machines couldn't cope with it.

William Forsyth, the *Journal* editor, must have had second thoughts about boosting the evening paper, for in the race for sales it soon began to show the morning paper a clean pair of heels. It is an intriguing thought that at one time serious consideration was given to closing down the *Journal* and leaving the field to the *Evening Express*. The *Journal*, struggling against fierce opposition from the *Free Press* saw its circulation drop below 10,000 copies by 1886. The directors called a meeting to discuss a proposal to shut down the morning paper and concentrate on the successful *Evening Express*. They decided against it.

In 1890, a lucky windfall saved the *Journal*. John Gray Chalmers, the last surviving great-grandson of the founder, James Chalmers, left the company £10,000 in his will, with instructions that it be invested in the paper's future. Half of this legacy was used to buy new premises in Broad Street and in May, 1894, the first papers were produced there.

The *Evening Express* continued to outstrip the *Journal* in sales. When the first world war broke out the evening paper sales totalled 45,500 a day, compared to the morning paper's 29,760. In the 1920s the *Journal's* circulation hovered between 15,000 and 20,000. The paper, it was said, was 'being carried by the *Evening Express*, which was outselling it five to one'. In 1922, the *Journal* amalgamated with the *Free Press* and the *Press and Journal* was born.

The financial picture was still bleak when the Canadian Roy Thomson bought Aberdeen Journals in 1959. A report drawn up for him showed that profits of £160,000 in 1956 had dropped to £80,000 in 1957 and plunged to £28,000 in 1958. The *Press and Journal,* selling at 2d, had a circulation of 89,000 a day, while the dearer threepenny *Evening Express* was selling 85,000. The Thomson Group's deputy managing director, meeting managers and trade union officials, told them that although the P&J's circulation looked healthy, it had been losing money for years. 'I think we're now at the point when the *Evening Express* cannot carry its elder brother any longer', he said.

Three years after 'Uncle Roy' took over the Aberdeen papers I became Editor of the *Evening Express*. It was the start of the Swinging Sixties – and the space age. In April, 1961, Yuri Alekseyevich Gagarin, son of a Russian carpenter, hurtled into the heavens in a space ship weighing more than four and a half tons – 'the Columbus of interplanetary space', Moscow Radio called him. 'I saw the earth from a great height', he reported. 'I could see seas, mountains, big cities, rivers and forests. The sky is very dark and the earth is blueish. Everything is clearly visible'. He did one complete circuit of the earth and landed at a prearranged spot 108 minutes later, decisively winning the long space-race with America.

The road to the planets was open, and less than ten years later the Americans took it. In July, 1969, astronaut Neil Armstrong descended from a lunar module called the Eagle and stepped on to the moon. A message went back to the earth – 'The Eagle has landed'. Millions of people gazing into the skies could scarcely believe that now there really *was* a man on the moon. About 5,000 people crowded London's Trafalgar Square to see the touchdown on a huge screen put up by Thames TV. A boy born in Fife during the night was named Neil Edwin Michael after Armstrong and his fellow-cosmonaut, Edwin Aldrin. Even today, moon-gazing, we can still barely believe that up on that shining yellow orb is a plaque carrying the inscription: 'Here men from the planet Earth first set foot upon the moon, July 1969, A.D. We came in peace for all mankind'. Back on old Mother Earth, Cliff Richard and the Shadows were singing 'I Could Easily Fall'.

The year 1963 – the year in which President John Kennedy was assassinated and the John Profumo/Christine Keeler scandal broke – Beatlemania swept the country. This is what the *Evening Express* had to say about it:

The Beatles are the first people to make rock 'n' roll respectable. They have won over the class snob, the intellectual snob, the grown-ups and the husbands.

They have a following in Balliol College, Oxford, and the Inns of Court; policemen, engaged to keep the bulging lines of fans off the stage, themselves gaze mesmerised while the crowds swell behind them; old men gape in wonder; cartoonists put them in political cartoons.

They say there has been nothing like it since Johnnie Ray; in fact there has been nothing like it ever. We've had idols before but we've never had four idols for the price of one.

In 1964, Aberdeen became Typhoid City, a pariah town nobody wanted to know. It all began with a 7lb. tin of bad corned beef from Argentina and it turned into an epidemic that put 500 people in hospital. The city's medical officer of health, Dr Ian A. G. MacQueen, called Aberdeen the Beleagured City – a quote that was splashed across the front page of the *Evening Express* and almost every other newspaper in the country.

Some newspapers, particularly foreign journals, went over the top. We became the City of Fear, a place where no one was allowed to enter or leave, where the dead lay in the streets and bodies were thrown into the sea. This kind of sensationalism had no place in a local paper, but the *Evening Express* nevertheless gave massive coverage to the story. We were the readers' link with reality. Even Wee Alickie had a role to play. The *Green Final* cartoon character, who for years had commented on the Dons performances at Pittodrie, got a free transfer to the news pages to urge Aberdonians to wash their hands.

One of the typhoid victims was Baillie Frank Magee, who many years later wrote about it in a series written for the *Evening Express*. Baillie Magee thought that Dr MacQueen's description of Aberdeen as 'a beleagured city' was the most emotive and possibly the most harmful phrase used by the MOH. 'We had now reached the stage when people would not phone Aberdeen and lorry drivers refused to deliver goods into the city. Life in the hospitals settled down to a pattern. I was fortunate in my friends, for they ran out of ideas for presents and brought in cans of beer and the odd half-bottle of whisky. In the next cubicle were a farmer from Banchory and an honours student from Greece and this unlikely trio had evening parties.'

Looking back on it, the real hero of the Aberdeen typhoid outbreak was chubby, balding, pipe-smoking Dr MacQueen, whose 'emotive' phrases were swallowed up by pressmen like hungry fish reaching for bait. He was always good for a headline, for he knew how important it was to get his message over to the public. He also knew when to hit out, as, for instance, when the *Evening Express* carried a letter from an angry mother whose schoolgirl daughter had been charged three pence for the use of a wash-basin in a public toilet at the Beach. What Wee Alickie, washing *his* hands, would have said about it can only be imagined. What the city's MOH said was clear enough. 'This letter', wrote Baillie Magee, 'was described by Dr MacQueen in invective worthy of 18th century Parliament'.

More than thirty years after the typhoid outbreak, an interesting footnote to it was given by William Deedes, former MP and cabinet minister and one-time editor if the *Daily Telegraph*. Lord Deedes, in his autobiography *Dear Bill*, published in 1997, told how, when an election was approaching and the Conservative Government was getting 'jumpier about small things', the Aberdeen epidemic set alarm bells ringing at Westminster. On a Sunday morning in June, 1964, Deedes got a call from the Prime Minister, Alec Douglas-Home, who was worried about a speech in which Harold Wilson had alleged that the Government had known since March about the corned beef being manufactured in Argentina without chlorinated water.

Later that day, Selwyn Lloyd, Leader of the House, rang Deedes to say that the Prime Minister had also been on to him about a typhoid story in the *Sunday Times*, and in yet another call to Deedes a man from the Ministry of Agriculture wanted to know, with 'a note of urgency in his voice', how he was to deal with inquiries about typhoid and the bully beef.

'Typhoid still haunting us', noted Deedes in mid-June. The truth about the typhoid scare, he said, was that a Ministry of Agriculture inspector on tour in South America had notified his department early in March that a plant in Argentina was not chlorinating its cooling water. A principal medical officer of health was informed. His view was that no further shipments should be accepted, but, as there had been no illness arising from this product, it would not be reasonable to have withdrawn stocks of corned beef from the plant which were already in circulation. 'It is not only facts that count', commented Deedes. 'Sometimes the interpretation put on facts matters as well'.

Two years later the Tories had more to worry about than corned beef. On Friday, 1 April, 1966, the *Evening Express* carried the banner headline – COASTING TO NO. 10, with the sub-heading, WIN OF THE CENTURY? Harold Wilson had won 'a triumphant – and massive – General Election victory'. But *Evening Express* readers knew the result before it was announced. They did it with an Election Bingo feature which followed the pattern of voting and predicted the final majority. Looking at the date, some readers might have thought that it was an April Fool's Day joke, but the results were remarkable. For instance, the BBC's predicted Labour majority at 11.25 pm on election night was 125 seats. The E.E. Bingo computer forecast was 126 seats.

What the computer could never have forecast was that close on fifty years of Conservative domination in South Aberdeen would be smashed. Lady Tweedsmuir, a stereotype Tory who had held the seat for twenty years, was out. To pressmen she had been an aloof and often unapproachable MP, and in her successor they saw a different type of politician. He was a 28-year-old Glasgow solicitor, living in a council house in Kincorth, who had never been inside the House of Commons even as a visitor. His name – Donald Dewar.

The picture in the *Evening Express's* Election Special showed Donald and his wife having a cup of tea after enjoying a dish of fish brought straight from the market as a tit-bit for the new MP's victory-morning breakfast. You look at the tall, gangling, bespectacled figure in the photograph – 'I'm about 6ft. 3in. when I remember to straighten up', he said – and think of the Donald Dewar of today, older, greyer, still stooping a little, voluble and full of confidence – the man who once said he would find the House of Commons 'a frightening experience'. It was said that if he lived up to the promise he had shown he would go far, which had a prophetic ring about it. He was to become Secretary of State of Scotland in Tony Blair's New Labour Government and the man who was to be marked out as first Leader of the new Scottish Parliament in Edinburgh.

So that was the Swinging Sixties, a decade of big news and big ideas. For me, twelve more turbulent years lay ahead in the Editor's chair, steering the 'Auld Express' into the seventies and eighties and into an era of new newspaper technology.

CHAPTER TEN

Bribing and Twisting

You cannot hope to bribe or twist,
thank God! the British journalist,
But, seeing what the man will do
unbribed, there's no occasion to.

Hanging from a wall in my house is a bronze replica of the front page of the Aberdeen *Evening Express*, dated 21 February, 1982, with a banner headline running across it proclaiming 'Twenty Not Out'. This was the page that was never seen by the paper's readers, for it was designed by my editorial staff and presented to me at a surprise party when I completed twenty years as editor of the paper.

It was written mostly in light-hearted vein (there was an advertisement on it which read, 'Tired? Listless? Depressed? Cancel your P&J now'), but it also drew attention to the fact that in my two decades as Editor I had raised the paper's daily sale to 'a spectacular 82,000 plus'. It mentioned, too, that I had once written a column, under the name Rex Baird, that had become 'the scourge of bureaucratic ineptitude in the fifties'.

'Ever ready to argue the toss when he believes he is right', it said, 'Bob in full flood is quite a spectacle'. It went on to recall what happened during a verbal encounter with a Grampian councillor during my editorship. My wife Sheila arrived at the office to pick me up and, climbing the stairs, found her way barred by members of the staff.

'There were people standing all the way upstairs with their heads to one side', she said, 'and more in the corridor outside his office. Bob was having an awful row with Sandy Mutch, the Convener of Grampian Region, and they all had their ears to the wall listening'.

Although I have forgotten what the argument was about, I remember that Councillor Mutch threatened to take the matter to higher authority, first to the managing director, then to the editorial director in London, and finally to Lord Thomson himself. With each step up the hierarchical scale I became more and more incensed. I said in no uncertain terms that he could take it to the Lord God above if he wanted to, but made it clear that it would make not the slightest difference. The result was stalemate, but after that our relationship was put on a more even keel.

The author and his wife Sheila with a mock front page of the *Evening Express*. It was produced by the staff to mark the Editor's twenty years in the editor's chair.

There was an amusing sequel to the Sandy Mutch row. When I had marked up twenty years in the Editor's chair, congratulations from fellow-editors in the Thomson group all over the country were read out at the celebration dinner. Humour and whisky featured in most of them. Bill Sinclair, a Scot who was editing the Middlesbrough evening paper, asked: 'How on earth do you do it, loon? Please tell us the secret – and the name of your Distiller!' Roy Lilley, in Belfast, wrote: 'I'm with you in spirit, and will have a quiet dram with the thought'. Ian Nimmo, Editor of the Edinburgh evening paper, wrote: 'Editing a newspaper is like making love to an elephant: if you do it right nothing happens for a very long time; if you do it wrong you get trampled to death'. Geoff Baylis, assistant managing editor in Middlesbrough, mentioned my colleague, Peter Watson, editor of the *Press and Journal,* who was a few years younger than myself. 'Is it really true that Peter Watson is your grand-dad?' he asked.

But the most unusual message came from a Mrs Oslena Stott. I had never heard of Mrs Stott. Her contribution, written in Biblical language, described how in 1962 the Lord God 'saw that the peoples of Aberdeen and all the tribes of Banff, Kincardine, Moray and Auchterturra were sinners of the most vile description' and smote them with a new Editor of the *Evening Express* called Bob Smith, who came down upon them like a thunder-clap. It told how he had 'taken unto himself the aura of the Almighty by saying 'Let there be dialysis machines, let there be a gynaecological laser, and yea let there by a whole body scanner'. And lo there *were* kidney machines, there *was* a gynaecological laser, and there *was* a whole body scanner.'

Mrs Stott also described how the new Editor had pursued men of power and influence – 'yea did he slam them, lash them, hammer them and rap them, yea even the Grampian Health Board, savagely diminishing them in the eyes of the lieges who hitherto had admired, respected and revered them as the repositories of all wisdom'. The *Evening Express* had made dreadful attacks and assaults on 'the leaders of the tribes, on the Town and County Councils which in turn begat the District and Regional Councils and their chief men and elders – *yea even Chairman Mutch.*'

Who was Oslena Stott? A religious maniac? A councillor writing under an assumed name? There were two clues. One was the use of the name 'Auchterturra', the other was a reference to 'Scotland the What?' as 'a limp so-called entertainment provided by three pathetic old men who should have been tending their gardens and washing their motor cars'. The writer, it turned out, was an employee of the Grampian Health Board who was better known in his 'Scotland the What?' role. 'Oslena' was Buff Hardie himself.

The Sandy Mutch incident was a mild example of the old 'bribe and twist' verse, although in this case it was 'twisting' only in the sense of exerting pressure. I encountered both bribing *and* twisting in my long newspaper career. As a raw young reporter covering the local police court, I was more than once offered a 'backhander' to keep someone's name 'oot o' the paper'. Some people thought this was a perfectly normal thing to do. 'Foo much is it tae keep it oot?' they would ask, reaching into their pockets. They were surprised and upset when the offer was turned down.

On the other hand, some people were prepared to 'bribe and twist' to get their names *into* the paper. Mostly, however, they did it by persuasion. Bulky, friendly 'G.R'. – G.R. M'Intosh, councillor and one-time joiner – handed out miniature samples of his work to reporters when he dropped into Broad Street for a chat with the boys. Another 'character' who cultivated the Press was the voluble Dick Gallagher, whose knowledge of Aberdeen drinking howffs led to

Robert Smith, Editor of the *Evening Express*, presents a crystal goblet to Aberdeen's Lord Provost, William Fraser, as a token of friendship in the paper's centenary year.

the publication of a guide-book on local pubs. There were also a number of 'rent a quote' councillors who were always ready to talk to the press. Others kept their lips sealed. In the days when the *Evening Express'* and *Press and Journal* were part of the Kemsley chain we were regarded as capitalist hirelings, sitting at our desks waiting for instructions from our Tory masters in London.

The man responsible for the 'bribe and twist' verse was Humbert Wolfe, who was born in 1886, died in 1940, and in between wrote a book of poetry called *The Uncelestial City.* The book was all about death, with the 'bribe and twist' verse thrown in almost as an aside. He had little good to say about the press: 'Some new sensation will be found to harrow the public in the morning, when it wakes', he grumbled. He would probably have agreed with Arnold Bennett, who believed that journalists 'say a thing they know isn't true, in the hope that if they keep on saying it long enough it will be true'. That may have had an element of truth in it, but on the whole it was an over-harsh criticism. Aberdonians half believed it but put it more succinctly: 'Jist dinna believe *a'thing* ye read in the papers'.

In the late 1950s, when I was Assistant Editor of the *Evening Express*, I started a column under the name of Rex Baird. The column was launched with the title REX BAIRD TALKING FRANKLY, with an overline saying 'The Saturday column with Pep and Punch'. Harrowing the public in the morning, maybe. This is what I wrote on Saturday, 11 July, 1959, at the start of Aberdeen's annual holiday:

You lucky people! Two weeks with nothing to do but laze in the sun and spend all your money. If you are sitting at home this Trades Fortnight you will no doubt be strolling down our magnificent new boulevard, which Councillor MacIver wants to call by the ugly name of 'Sea Gate'.

'Boulevard' is no use, he feels, because there are no trees.

Why not plant some, Councillor?

Never mind, once you pass the sea gate, what wonders lie beyond!

For instance, on one part of the beach, children can play happily among the barbed wire which still sticks up through the sand, left there as an interesting relic of a war that ended fourteen years ago.

We must give them time, you know . . .

Then, for the fascination of visitors and stay-at-homes, there is the thrill of the BIG JUMP. You will find it at the entrance to the beach – a big slab of semi-circular concrete that leads to the sands.

Between the edge of this base and the actual beach is a drop of, say, 3ft. 6in., which is a tidy step down – or up!' – for those who are not so young.

Of course, you can always do a balancing act on the water pipe that sticks out from the base. This will help you to rise to the occasion . . . maybe!

Thousands of people flock to the sands – and there are only twenty-six chalets available. Ayr, with a population of just over 45,000, has more than twice that number – and they don't have black tarred roofs and cream walls. Aberdeen should have a beach to match its boulevard. It's time someone got cracking!

Despite Councillor MacIver's objections, the name 'boulevard' stayed and the 'sea gate' plan was blown away by the snell winds that came whistling down the prom. Nowadays, the idea of thousands of people flocking to the sands *and* sitting in chalets with black tarred roofs sounds like something out of a journalist's fevered imagination. It is a pity Rex Baird is no longer around to pass judgement on the Beach as it is today.

'Talking Frankly' became a popular Saturday feature on a day when newspaper sales tended to drop. It tilted at bureaucracy, criticised backward hotel owners, spotlighted complaints about mothers taking four-year-old boys into the women's section of the Bon-Accord Baths, warned about cars being allowed into the Duthie Park – 'Cars and more cars! Big cars and little cars!

INSIDE the park!' – and told about folk in Northfield and Mastrick who couldn't get up council house stairs because there were no banisters.

It drew attention to an Aberdeen doctor who kept a woman and child sitting on the doorstep outside his surgery until he could see them. It also turned the spotlight on a kirk that charged old-age pensioners for the use of a hall when it lay empty during the summer months. The matter was passed on to the treasurer, John Slessor, but with no success. 'Mr Slessor made no bones about it', said Rex Baird. 'He said he didn't want to see me, he didn't like the press, and as far as he was concerned I couldn't leave too soon.'

Then there was the case of the unknown Lord Provost. This is how it began:

'Girls, you should be ashamed of yourselves!'

'An alderman from Wallasey was shopping in a big Union Street store when he casually asked an assistant the name of the city's Lord Provost.

'She could not tell him and went off to consult another girl.

Still no satisfaction.

'She had to ask two more girls before she could answer the Englishman's query. He was not very impressed.

'I think Lord Provost Stephen should invite you to the Town House for one of his well-known cuppas – and to tell you a little about who runs our city and how they do it.

The provost they didn't know, George Stephen, was a postie-poet who wrote couthy poems about Aberdeen, so perhaps it wasn't surprising that young shop girls weren't aware of his existence. Yet the best-remembered provosts have been the couthy ones, civic leaders like Tommy Mitchell, who called the Royal Princesses 'quinies', and Alex Collie, who was liked and respected despite his occasionally tortured Aberdeen accent. Mrs Collie, an ordinary Aberdeen 'wifie', was asked to open an annual Christmas film show which the *Evening Express* held in the Odeon for old-age pensioners. She was a shy woman and didn't want to face the public, but I gave her a helping hand and she brought the house down. After that, she did it willingly, but only if I was at her side.

Mrs Collie, of course, was the Lady Provost. The original title for the Lord Provost's wife was 'The Lord Provost's-lady of Aberdeen'. In 1996 confusion was arose when a lady became the First Citizen – and was immediately called *Lord* Provost. I have never been able to understand how a Lord could be made a Lady by a stroke of the civic pen. At anyrate, Lord Provost Margaret Farquhar will almost certainly be remembered, if only for a heading which appeared in the *Evening Express*. 'The Bionic Provost' it said. This was when Mrs Farquhar was having hip trouble – 'It really wis affa sair', she said. She was was given a hip replacement and after it said she was going to offer herself to Aberdeen F.C. as a star player – 'the bionic woman!'

Looking at the Rex Baird column forty years later, I find that its style and

Bob Smith (right) and William Forsyth, assistant managing director, with an 'E.E.' birthday cake made for the centenary of the paper.

content carry faint echoes of long ago. It had the same abrasive approach to stories that were the hallmark of two magazines published in Aberdeen in the 1880s – the *Northern Figaro* and the *Bon-Accord*. Before that, a number of scurrilious magazines dabbled in malicious gossip about local people, but the *Figaro* and the *Bon-Accord*, were in a different class.

Donald J. Withrington, reader in Scottish History at Aberdeen University, mentioned these magazines in *The City and its Worlds,* a collection of studies of Aberdeen. He thought that the *Bon-Accord* was closer to the local political scene than the *Northern Figaro* ('It was full of in-jokes about the councillors', he said) and it was less aggressive than the *Figaro*, although it had its own style of cutting commentary. 'That Aberdeen should spawn two substantial journals of this kind is itself notable,' he said.

The birthday cake made for the centenary of the *Evening Exoress*.

In 1881, the *Figaro* raised its voice about the town's health and the state of its slums. It warned that the council was likely to become the most extravagant of modern times, forever finding 'new ways of spending the citizen's money'. In 1886, the *Bon-Accord* entered the fray.

The writers had a wide choice of targets, firing broadsides wherever their fancy took them. In May, 1887, a few potshots were aimed at Queen Victoria, or, at anyrate, at her Jubilee celebrations. According to *Figaro*, the Jubilee put a tremendous strain on 'that most unhappy class of men – editors'. Someone suggested that they mark the Jubilee by giving away 3,000 florins. *Figaro* thought this idea was 'quite good enough', but it poured scorn on another proposal that the coins be kept as ornaments.

Jubilee day in Aberdeen was Saturday, June 18, and in that month's issue of the *Figaro* a letter appeared pointing out that the Queen had 'gotten her face washed', presumably in readiness for the celebrations, but it was Victoria's statue, not the Queen in the flesh, who was given a clean-up. 'They tell me her claes got a rub down at the same time', wrote the correspondent. 'Fa ever did it was surely ill aff for soap. Ye widna think that there was an Ogston ('Soapy' Ogston's factory in the Gallowgate) and some mair o' them makin' it'. His parting shot was that 'they micht give "Prince" at the corner o' Union Terrace a dicht at the same time'.

Mostly, however, the magazines concentrated on council affairs. In December, 1888, the *Bon-Accord* said in a leader that it would never descend to scurrility, but would dish up fun and 'keep the pot bilin'' with topics of the day. It kept the pot boiling by attacking councillors for their behaviour at a meeting to discuss a new road to the Links. Cries of 'You're a humbug!' and 'Wisdom in big heads!' were hurled about, and the *Bon-Accord* said that if the council were to 'show the way in the morals and manners business' it was 'high time that certain members were supplied with a new vocabulary'.

The treasurer had been criticised the previous month for *his* careless use of words. 'He is a plain man and speaks plainly', said the *Bon-Accord*, but it was going rather too far when he dubbed Mr Pringle as 'Mr What's-his-Name – Mr Rubislaw'. Epithets like these are not conducive to future brotherly love.

Alongside the Victorian greybeards was a young councillor called Lyon, whose name kept popping up in the pages of both the *Figaro* and the *Bon-Accord* in the late eighties. The *Northern Figaro* had doubts about his future. Councillor Lyon became involved in an argument with a Major Crombie at a council meeting to discuss testing the St Nicholas bells in Louvain in Belgium. He declared that 'the Major's remarks were only to be expected from one who was connected with a weekly paper that had tried to hold him [Mr Lyon] up to ridicule.'

It turned out that Councillor Lyon had got his facts wrong. The weekly paper was the *Figaro*, whose editor made it clear that 'the gallant Major' had no connection with it or with what appeared in it. It said that if there were many scenes like the one at the council meeting there would be a long farewell to Councillor Lyon's popularity as a member of the council and a representative of the community. He should never allow himself to blurt out what he might have to retract and feel sorry for the next moment. 'Until he learns this all-important lesson of judiciousness', declared *Figaro*, 'Councillor Lyon must of necessity ever remain a Councillor who, however much he may be impressed with his own importance as such, can never reach a high point as a public man.'

The Bells Committee of the Town Council decided to send two members to Louvain to watch and report on the tuning of the St Nicholas bells. They were Councillor Lyon, who was convener of the committee, and Councillor

A HUNNER years has been the stint,
Sin' first ye started up in print;
An' since the day ye did begin't
Ye've seen success –
Sae here's tae the neist five score you'll rin't,
The auld 'Express'.

Your prent for common-weal aye use –
In black an' white air a' your views –
Whiles tae instruct an' whiles amuse,
An' ne'er be blate;
Tae trumpet Truth in a' your news,
Ye Fourth Estate!

Syne a' oor blessings we maun gie,
Tae match the daily worth o' thee:
Tae nourish aye a Press that's free
We sair hae need –
As lang as Truth sall bear the gree.
An' men can read

Andy Stewart's poem, written for the hundredth birthday of the 'Auld Express'.

Rust, and with them went ex-Baillie George Walker and Mr John Kirby, a professor of music, who was the council's expert. The *Figaro* saw the Louvain visit as nothing more than 'a nice little trip' for the trio. Lyon was the son of a hide and tallow merchant in George Street and the paper asked: 'What on earth does a hide and tallow merchant, an architect, or a teacher of music (professor, if you like the title better) know about bells? Is it not a little too much risk to send over three so unsophisticated mortals upon this mission of sound?

'Just let me see what these three know about campanology. In the hide and tallow business I am not aware that the subject of bells ever enters, so I shan't go further to prove Councillor Lyon's incompetence. As an architect, Councillor Rust may have drawn plans for a steeple to hold the bell or bells (I know not), but I am perfectly satisfied that about the bells he knows absolutely nothing, so that he doesn't count. Then, as to Mr Kirby, I have never heard of his having had any practical knowledge of bells or bell-founding, so that I am reluctantly obliged to chuck him between his companions. What in the world would be the use of sending this trio over for the purpose of hearing the bells tuned?

'I can quite understand and appreciate the motive which prompts the Bells Committee to send two of their number, but *what* in the name of wonder is the good of sending people with about as much knowledge of music as an old boot to take the bells off the hands of these foreign 'founders'? I have no hesitation in saying that the money spent on this deputation might as well be thrown into the dock.'

Despite *Figaro's* objections, the deputation went to Belgium in April and came back with the news that there was little wrong with the bells. Only minor changes would be required. The members also reported that they had been invited to Malines, where by special permission of the Burgomaster a carillon was played for three hours in their honour. As *Figaro* had said, 'A nice little trip'.

On 11 May the St Nicholas bells arrived back in Aberdeen and were drawn in triumph through the main streets of the city before being taken to St Nicholas Tower. There were no more attacks from the *Figaro* – and the *Bon-Accord* had the last word on the affair. Its 'Will o' the Wisp' column carried a tribute to Councillor Lyon – 'the Wonderful Councillor' it called him. He would, it said, 'be made glad at last – the bells in St Nicholas Tower are really a very fine lot indeed. In the face of all that has been said, done, and written over these hitherto muchly-abused campanological specimens, Mr Lyon can afford a tiny grin of satisfaction'.

The Wonderful Councillor's grin must have broadened when he remembered *Figaro's* warning that unless he changed his ways he would 'never reach a high point as a public man'. In fact, Alexander Lyon became leader of what was known as 'The Young Party' in the town council and was appointed Lord Provost in 1905. He played a leading role in the laying-out of the Stewart, Walker and Westburn Parks and of the Union Terrace Gardens, in the widening of Union Bridge and in the clearing away of slum areas in the Gallowgate and Exchequor Row.

He was knighted by Edward VII in September, 1906, when the King and Queen Alexandra came to the city for the quater-centenary celebrations of Aberdeen University. His long and memorable term of office ended in 1908, when he retired from the Council. He died in 1927. As for the fiery *Figaro*, it went the way of many of the weekly papers that were published at the end of the nineteenth century. The *Bon-Accord* outlived its rival, running on until it was closed by a strike in 1959.

CHAPTER ELEVEN

The Bangkok Affair

> What business has the vulgar rabble
> To ken what's done at Council table?
> The wheels are aye kept tight and greasy,
> And Councillors ride soft and easy.

Aberdonians faced life with an alcoholic hiccup in the good old days. In the late eighteenth and early nineteenth centuries the city was saturated with clubs and societies whose members imbibed as if there was no tomorrow. There were drinking howffs in plenty, among them nine mason's lodges and the halls of a host of opulent friendly societies. There was a medical society whose members 'discussed more than dry bones' and a philosophical society whose solemn discussions became less dry as the evening wore on.

They called it the age of conviviality. At elections, by all accounts, everyone was 'thoroughly soaked'. Bachelors and benedicts wined and dined in style, shipmasters, dyers and wigmakers saw the evening out 'with decent mirth and hilarity', and the Incorporated Trades offered 'sevenfold hospitality' to all the notables in Aberdeen. There was talk of loosening the neckties of those who fell under the table.

George Walker, in his *Aberdeen Awa'*, published in 1897, said that all ranks and classes 'formed themselves into congenial coteries, meeting in inns at all seasons and hours'. Had the modern reporter been in existence then, he added, 'what a flood of light been would have been thrown on the social life of the period'.

One thing the modern reporter would have noticed was the lack of restraint among the City Fathers. There were not many baillies or councillors who turned away from the temptation of strong drink. John Home, the Keeper of the Town House, was heard to sing a ditty which went:

> In guid times an auld, when days were cauld,
> Wi' sleet an' sna' and a' that,
> The Council board was aye weel stored
> Wi' something nice and a' that,
> An' a' that an' a' that,
> Wi' sherry, port an' a' that'.

When any business was to be discussed the city purse was available at the drop of a hat. It was freely drawn on for conviviality – in the eyes of drouthy councillors there was nothing worse than a 'stingy Treasurer'. Walker said that in the eighteenth century town councils managed to mix private pleasures with public duties much more than would be considered proper in the nineteenth century. Some people would argue that there was a return to the old ways in the twentieth century.

'Drink', wrote Walker, 'was the accompaniment of births, marriages and funerals, of every business transaction, every rise in life, and almost every gathering. On the founding of any building, and the completion of every work, drink money was always looked for over and above the regular payment.'

By the turn of the century there were signs of a decline in 'clubbing', although the drinking went on. In 1807, the Revd James Hall wrote in his book, *Travels in Scotland*, that Aberdonians were remarkably hospitable in their own houses, but still kept up with the fashion of periodical clubs. 'Some of them', he said, 'meet together like the common tradesmen of London at a public house every night.'

The amount of liquor consumed in the age of conviviality was staggering. People's capacity was measured not by glasses, but by bottles. Three-bottle men were common. They thought no more of two bottles of port than of two cups of tea – and there were some who could tuck six bottles under their belt. A tale was told of 'a dreadful day' at Brechin Castle in 1804 when seven men drank thirty-one bottles of red champagne, besides Burgundy and other concoctions.

For many years, Aberdeen councillors, like those in other burghs, found a ready source of free liquor and good food in the annual inspection of municipal undertakings. In these ritual outings the state of the gas-works or water-works took second place to the quality of the food and drink that rounded them off. Dig deep into the council minutes of a century ago and you will find the name of a heroic figure who tried to prevent this civic lurch into drink and gluttony.

On 10 July, 1888, eighteen members of the Water Committee of Aberdeen Town Council met to discuss the annual inspection of the City Waterworks. Councillor John Rust moved that the inspection take place on Saturday, July 28, and Baillie Daniel Mearns seconded the motion. Then Councillor Alexander Cook dropped a bombshell into the proceedings. He wanted to wipe out the old tradition. He put forward an amendment 'that the proposed inspection do not take place'. Instead, he told the shocked committee, a report should 'be procured from the Burgh Surveyor, or other competent person, as to the condition of the Waterworks'. He was seconded by Councillor George Maconnachie.

Two other members, Councillors Crombie and Moir, added their names to the amendment, but it was defeated by fourteen votes to four. Councillor Cook registered his dissent. At a meeting of the Council on August 20 a report was submitted saying that the inspection of the City Waterworks had taken place and members of the Council had 'found the works in a satisfactory condition'. There was no comment on the condition of the councillors.

The dry official language of bureaucracy gives no indication of the turmoil Councillor Cook's amendment caused, but the controversy didn't end with his defeat. He made sure that the cost of his fellow-members' wining and dining was made public. On 22 December, the *Bon-Accord* newspaper carried a report which congratulated Councillor Cook on 'the plucky manner in which he made the powers-that-be disgorge the bills in connection with the late Waterworks Inspection'. It went on to say that these detailed accounts were unpleasant to 'certain sitting members', but the public had a right to know. The *Bon-Accord* published the details – in rhyme:

> If you wish just to peep at the Town
>   Council billing,
> Take thirty-six lunches, per head
>   price one shilling
> And twenty-four dinners that cost
>   eight and six
> (A sum which would keep all our poor
>   ones for weeks),
> Three bottles of claret and five of
>   old sherry,
> Each costing five shillings – exorbitant
>   very;
> Plus eleven – each costing nine bob – of
>   cham.,
> And ten of old whisky – a very good dram -
> And thirty good shillings for three of
>   old brandy –
> Fit nectar I wot for the veriest dandy;
>   The whisky at five and the brandy at ten -
> And aerated waters for the temperance men;
>   Such a nice little bill, as all will agree,
> For a Town Council drink at a Waterwork
>   spree!

The whisky-drinking, sherry-sipping councillors had already been upset by another of Councillor Cook's tactics. He threatened to have a photograph taken of them when they came back from their spree, either because he wanted their faces shown to the ratepayers or because he thought that some of them were unsteady on their feet. At any rate, as the *Bon-Accord,* observed, 'that must have made one or two councillors squirm and shrivel up a bit, we fancy.'

The *Bon-Accord* had a final piece of advice for councillors going to inspect the water-works in the future. 'Stick to that liquid which they inspect', it said, 'to wit, caul' water'.

If Councillor Cook's admendment had been accepted, no one knows what might have happened. Future committees *might* have stuck to caul' water, a new precedent *might* have been set, and old habits *might* have died with the passing of the century. Of course, that didn't happen. Nothing changed. The wheels were aye kept tight and greasy, as the old poem said, and councillors rode soft and easy . . .

Towards the end of the twentieth century the perks and 'freebies' were still there, and all through the country the faint odour of sleaze was permeating the town halls. In Aberdeen, people grumbled about free meals and drinks for councillors, about free parking places while ratepayers were filling up parking meters, about the use of Common Good funds, about lavish civic functions, and about councillors going off on questionable trips to faraway places at the ratepayers' expense.

When a deputation went to Louvain in Belgium to check the St Nicholas bells in 1887, the *Northern Figaro* said scornfully that it was nothing more than 'a nice little trip' for councillors. Almost a century later, another 'nice little trip' created an even greater furore. This time, the councillors were going on a much longer trip – to Bangkok!

It came to be known as the Bangkok Affair. It started in April, 1966, when Councillor J.S.G. Munro, a Tory standing under the name of Progressive, criticised Aberdeen Corporation's spending on conferences and trips abroad. He had been complaining for some time about ratepayers' money being wasted in this way. In the summer of 1966, Sweden, Denmark, Spain and Belgium were to be visited by Aberdeen town councillors and officials, with ratepayers footing the bill. In 1965, twenty-three representatives of the town council made trips to Regensburg, Jersey, Washington, Monaco, Paris, Belgrade, Dublin, Denmark, Belfast and Czechoslovakia at a cost of nearly £3,000.

Added to these trips were inspections, deputations, conferences, meetings of institutions and professional bodies, and business meetings in the United Kingdom. The bill for some 700 journeys was £10,676, an increase in travelling expenses from £6,369 in 1963 and £6,193 in 1960. It was, Councillor Munro told a meeting of the town council, 'high time this caper of jaunting round Europe and other countries was stopped'. Did the city get value for the money spent in this way? Were *all* these journeys really necessary?

I set out to find the answers to these questions in Newsprobe, a feature which went behind the news headlines to examine in greater depth local controversies and issues of importance. In it, Councillor Munro described the increase in foreign travel by council representatives as 'alarming'. Newsprobe, having sifted evidence from a variety of sources, recorded an 'open verdict'. There were, it said, reasonable arguments for and against the expenditure involved, but while there was doubt the council should deliberate very carefully before deciding who to send where.

Less than three weeks later, the council decided to send Treasurer Robert S. Lennox to Bangkok to a Congress of the International Union of Local Authorities. Baillie George Roberts, 'father' of the town council, said in an interview with the *Evening Express* that Aberdeen ratepayers should rise up in revolt against the move. It was, he said, a sheer waste of public money.

Edinburgh decided not to send a representative to Bangkok. An official of the town clerk's department said it had been found from previous conferences of this body they were 'not worth the time spent at them'. Dundee rejected the invitation. 'The idea was too daft for words', said Dundee's Labour Treasurer, Harry Dixon. In late May, William Ross, the Scottish Secretary, acted on council trips abroad. He told Glasgow Corporation that only two councillors should be sent on a ten-day tour of Scandinavia to study industrialised building. The council had intended sending four councillors. Aberdeen had also planned to send four councillors to Scandinavia, but two Progressive councillors declined to go.

Meanwhile, the Battle of Bangkok raged on in the letter columns of the *Evening Express*. A holiday at ratepayers' expense . . . a sheer waste of public money . . . a journey that wasn't really necessary . . . the letters poured in. 'What value will the city get for this expensive trip to the Far East?' asked one reader. 'Plans for a few pagodas to be built in the Duthie and Westburn Parks?' 'Join the Town Council and see the World!' said another, while a third sent up the cry, 'Oh for a town council of truly business people'. On and on it went . . . and the mass of mail received by the *Evening Express* was almost totally opposed to the Bangkok trip.

Treasurer Robert Lennox was twice given space in the *Evening Express* to state his case in detail, and the Newsprobe report made it clear that no one regarded the controversy as in any sense a personal reflection on the treasurer. It was the least that could be said about a man who was described by an opposition *Tory* councillor, Frank Magee, as 'a sea-green incorruptible'. Sadly, the treasurer still thought that the issue had 'strong anti-Lenox overtones'.

On Friday, 27 May, just prior to the town council meeting where a final decision would be taken on the Bangkok issue, I wrote a leader saying: 'CALL IT OFF!' Aberdeen ratepayers, I said, had shown that they were violently opposed to their money being spent on such an excursion. 'No one will lose in stature by facing up to facts and bowing to public opinion. There is a genuine and growing concern over trips abroad by local authority representatives.'

The council meeting was on Monday afternoon and I knew that strong

Treasurer LENNOX

The Bangkok Row

Edinburgh, Dundee . . . now Aberdeen has decided not to send a representative to the congress of the International Union of Local Authorities at Bangkok next February.

The decision was taken at a meeting of Aberdeen Town Council where the "Evening Express" came in for some sharp criticism.

This newspaper was accused by Treasurer R. S. Lennox, who was nominated for the Bangkok visit, of "creating an artificial campaign against the trip and trying to intimidate the Corporation."

Other Press critics were Councillors Andrew Forman and James A. Lamond (Lab.) and Frank Magee (Prog.). Councillors J. S. G. Munro, the Progressive leader, observed that when certain persons get into awkward situations they beat the Press as hard as they could.

Councillor MUNRO

THE TRIP IS OFF

. . . And 'Evening Express' comes under fire

AFTER a 40-minute discussion Aberdeen Town Council agreed that Treasurer Robert S. Lennox should not go to Bangkok to represent the city at the congress of the International Union of Local Authorities.

The council unanimously accepted an amendment from Treasurer Lennox himself that the city should not participate in the congress.

Treasurer Lennox said they had a Labour group meeting last Friday. They had not hidden and would not hide the fact that they held these meetings.

"Had there not been this artificially-created campaign we would have conducted our business in the ordinary way as we are elected to do and as we have an absolute right to do, and we would have come to our decision." he said.

"I think I am speaking for the whole of the corporation when I say there is strong resentment at the Press's attempt to intimidate this corporation on the decisions which are to be taken."

At this point he was interrupted by Councillor A. F. Mutch who said: "I dissociate myself from these remarks."

Treasurer Lennox: "You would, of course."

DICTATORSHIP

in conferences only 1/5 goes towards the cost.

"Yet, we are accused of being extravagant and wasteful."

The treasurer obviously referring to a Page One opinions piece on Friday, said that in this article the Press even had the audacity to claim that they started this off. This was not started with the recent campaign, but they say its roots go a little deeper to the previous month.

The question of participation in congresses of this sort was determined by the corporation on general principle in December, 1960, and not by the Press.

SCANDINAVIA

The treasurer then went on to deal with the visits to Scandinavia by two councillors and two officials.

The representation had not

Councillor HATCH

or whether they were so inward-looking that they thought councillors got no

regarded the counter-argument that no one would come to Aberdeen unless they went to Bangkok as so much nonsense.

"I, for my part, am grateful to the Press for highlighting this matter. I cannot say that I speak for all the ratepayers, any more than Councillor Forman can, but no doubt the public at large are very grateful indeed to the attention which has been directed to this matter."

He paid tribute to the amount of time spent by Treasurer Lennox on corporation business and if it had been within their power to give him some kind of reward they would have done so. But they did not think this Bangkok trip was intended as a personal reward.

Treasurer Lennox, replying, said: "I have never looked upon this proposal as anything personal. I am not looking for rewards in any form for myself in so far as my public work is concerned."

MONOPOLY

The *Evening Express*: End of the Bangkok Affair.

words would be said about the part played by the *Evening Express* in the controversy. I planned to get as much as I could into the the last edition of the paper. The reporters were briefed to send back their copy from the Town House in short 'takes'. I was standing by the sub-editors' desk when the first 'take' arrived. The balloon had gone up!

An artificially-created campaign . . . strong resentment at the Press attempt to intimidate this corporation . . . dictation by a non-elected body who said that the ratepayers had spoken . . . a headline saying 'Call it off. We are telling you to call it off' . . . a serious challenge'. Treasurer Lenox had come out with all guns firing. If they decided not to go, he said, it would be said they were cowards and falling down in front of public opinion. And if they decided to go to the congress then they would turn round and say 'You are flouting the decision of the people of Aberdeen'. Do you say that the corporation should meet under such duress to consider matters of this sort?

Councillor J.S.G. Munro, the Progressive leader, rejected the intimidation charge: 'When certain persons at certain times get into an awkward situation they automatically turn and beat the Press as hard as they can and accuse it of gross bias, unfair duress and any other accusation which occurs to them at the time', he said. They all tended to be critical of the press when they happened to express a view different from one's own but when they expressed one's view better than one could oneself, then they were all that was good.

The last 'take' came in time to catch the Late Final edition of the paper. Treasurer Lennox had moved an amendment to the Lord Provost Committee's original recommendation that he should represent the city at the Congress. The amendment said simply: 'We don't participate in the Congress at Bangkok'. The last edition went out with the banner headline: 'IT'S OFF!: NO VISIT TO BANGKOK'.

So that was the end of the Bangkok Affair. I was glad that the council had taken what I thought was the right decision, but I was also glad that it was all over, partly, I think, because I had considerable respect for the man at the centre of the controversy – the 'sea-green incorruptible' Treasurer Lennox. He may have been enigmatic, as Frank Magee had said, and possibly a little introverted, but I believed him to be a man of principle. He went on to serve two terms as Lord Provost of Aberdeen, with his wife Evelyn by his side, and it was during this time that I came to know Bert Lennox well.

Not long after I retired, BBC Scotland ran a programme about my newspaper career. It began against the familiar background roar of printing presses, with presenter Eric Crockart speaking about 'the start of the newspaper print run, the warning klaxon, the tremor underfoot as the great presses rumble into life . . . guaranteed to set the printer's ink racing through the veins of every true newspaper man'. Then it introduced me as one of Britain's longest-serving evening paper editors. In the programme, the story of the Bangkok Affair was told and Treasurer Lennox – 'the man who didn't go to Bangkok', said Crockart – was interviewed. 'Despite the standpoint of the *Evening Express* in the affair', said Eric, 'he was to become firm friends with Bob Smith'. This is what the former Treasurer said:

I had quite a regard for Bob in his editorial years. It was during that time, particularly in the second occasion that I was Lord Provost, that we became closer together, with a mutual respect. During his period of editorship he was very fair.

This may be difficult to understand, but I didn't subscribe to personal matters in local government. It was always the issue, it was always the principle, it was always the policy, these were the things that mattered to me. It was the substance that was important, not the person.

I think that he is totally reliable, that he is non-aggressive on a personal level, and that he has a fair degree of justice in most of the things that he says and does. I like him as a person.

It was an accolade that I greatly appreciated. The sounds of the Battle of Bangkok seemed far away then.

CHAPTER TWELVE
Ghosts

A planner's space-age dream took shape in Aberdeen thirty years ago. It envisaged a huge skyscraper city rising 4,000 feet above the ground. It was to be twenty times higher than the new municipal offices built near its base . . . and it would be almost the height of Ben Nevis. Inside it, 25,000 people would live out their lives in an environment that might have belonged to science fiction.

This was the Aberdeen of the future as seen in a sketch by Iain Ramsay, a graduate student at the Scott Sutherland School of Architecture. It appeared in a series of articles which I ran in the *Evening Express* in 1969 with the help of the school. The title of the series was 'Aberdeen 2000 AD'.

The idea of skyscraper cities came from Robert Gabriel, a German engineer, who in 1964 forecast that 'the rapid and increasing horizontal expansion of towns and cities would result in the eventual sacrifice of the whole countryside for building purposes'. He thought that the solution lay in the design of a self-contained skyscraper city. Its upper storeys would have a diameter of 210 feet and would accommodate 8,000 houses, while in the lower storeys, with a diameter of 600 feet, there would be factories, offices and business and cultural amenities.

High-speed lifts would shoot people up to the top of the skyscraper and moving pedestrian walkways would take them to any part of the building. There would be schools, shopping precincts, libraries, indoor parks and amusement areas. There would also be churches, hospitals, sanatoriums and outdoor recreational facilites – golf courses, tennis courts, horse-racing tracks, and football pitches. In Aberdeen, an area bounded by Union Street, Bridge Street, Guild Street and Market Street would be required to form the base of the skyscraper city.

Iain Ramsay's sketch provided a bird's-eye view of the skyscraper. From it, prominent city landmarks could be picked out . . . the Town House, ships in the harbour, HM Theatre, the Beach, the Market Cross in the Castlegate – and another more familiar skyscraper. This was the multi-storey Marischal Court, a midget 'skyscraper' compared with its Big Brother. It was said that eight skyscraper cities would accommodate the whole population of Aberdeen, and it was anticipated that cities of this kind would be built in ever growing

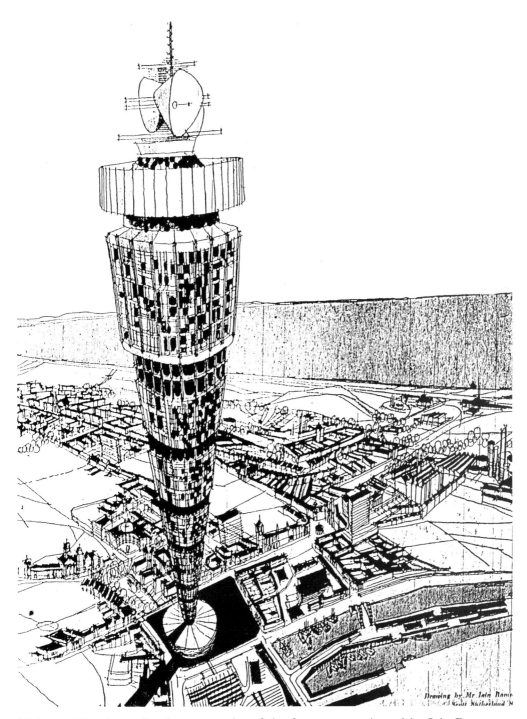

This was Aberdeen, the skyscraper city of the future, as envisaged by Iain Ramsey, a graduate student at the Scott Sutherland School of Architecture, as part of an 'Aberdeen 2000' feature in 1969.

numbers in the year 2000 AD. Thirty years later, Aberdeen's first skyscraper city remains firmly rooted in Fantasy Land.

So just how accurate were the *Evening Express* crystal-gazers in 1969? Looking at their predictions three decades later, they seem to have been reasonably near the mark. One man who hit the target was Stanley Wilkinson, head of the Scott School of Architecture, who wrote about the sociological and economic factors that would affect developments thirty years ahead. He believed that between 1970 and 2000 AD the status of family life would decline. It was anticipated that in Aberdeen only one quarter of the householders would have children living at home. He wrote:

In 2000 AD boys and girls leaving school at the age of seventeen years will live in their own flats, and in consequence of this kind of social movement more and more older people will be living alone. By 2000 AD women will be completely emancipated and they will take an equal share with men in the social scene whilst holding important posts in commerce and industry. Such a society will demand greater provision of nursery schools, group restaurants, welfare evening classes and older people's homes and clubs.

As teenagers start their own homes at younger ages than hitherto and women participating in activities which have until recently been the prerogative of men, the traditional model of family life will be replaced by a kind of society which will have a moral standard of behaviour unfamiliar to that of today.

That picture of a changing Aberdeen came close to reality towards the end of the twentieth century. If our Scott Sutherland crystal-gazers had been able to peer into the twenty-first century they might have seen a bleaker picture . . . a nightmare scenario, perhaps, yet one that many people had anticipated and feared. They would have been looking at a city strangled by its own traffic. They would have seen Aberdeen in the grip of rampant drug addiction. Their crystal ball would have thrown back pictures of empty churches and old historic kirks turned into snack bars, nightclubs, offices and flats. Stanley Wilkinson's 'moral standard of behaviour' would have reached rock bottom.

What, then, *does* the new Millenium hold for the once-booming oil city? Edward Parham, Principal Lecturer in Planning at the Scott Sutherland School, took a look at the growing problem of traffic in the 'Aberdeen 2000' survey. The background to his report was a city ugly with double yellow lines and prodded into a reluctant acceptance of park-and-ride schemes that many people didn't want, partly because they preferred to use their own cars, partly because they didn't want *their* streets turned into park-and-ride routes. Householders raised petitions against them, and every day a great convoy of commuter cars choked the roads into the town. But we were well warned about

Lord Provost William Fraser was the front seat passenger in this vintage car during a Vintage Car Rally organised by the *Evening Express*.

it. A headline in the *Evening Express* in 1969 read: 'Choke up! If you think traffic is bad now, just wait!'

Edward Parham said that in 1969 one family in three owned a car; by the year 2000 almost every family in Britain would possess one – and many would have more than one. 'Wars have destroyed cities', he declared. 'The motor vehicle, if not controlled, will destroy more effectively and more permanently than shells and bombs.'

He put forward two main solutions. The first was to ban motor cars from city centres and replace them on a large scale with improved means of public transport. That policy now seems to be foremost in the minds of the local authority, but many people regard the present public transport system as totally inadequate. The second solution was a startling one – a policy of complete freedom for the motor car. It would be extremely expensive and would involve 'a complex system of multi-lane and double-decker motorways flanked by gigantic parking areas and car stacks, the new cathedrals of the motor age'.

Here we are back in Fantasy Land. It is highly unlikely that canny Aberdonians would plump for such way-out plans. Most cities of the size of Aberdeen, said Parham, would be extremely cautious about plunging into untried and revolutionary means of transportation, so that the emphasis would probably be on restrictive measures as far as the private motorist was concerned, and on improving existing methods of public transport.

Then there was the drugs threat. In 1970, the year after the 'Aberdeen 2000' series appeared, the *Evening Express* took its own peep into the future – and was accused of scaremongering. On Monday, 9 November, the front page of the paper carried an 'Our View' with the headline 'Drugs in Aberdeen – facing the facts'. The drugs menace was beginning to raise its head in the city. There were reports of youths being fined for possessing drugs – and in the spring of that year Aberdeen City Police formed a drugs squad.

Because of this we ran a series of articles on drug-taking and drug-trafficking in Aberdeen and the North-east. Superintendent Bill Adams, head of Aberdeen CID, told us: 'Investigation about drugs has been a feature of 1970 and there is every indication that it will continue to increase'. But there were people who wanted to brush it under the carpet. It could never happen in Aberdeen, they said. One anonymous reader, signing himself 'Fair Play', took the *Evening Express'* to task for 'exaggerating a situation out of all proportions'. The writer, believed to be a student, claimed that we were being socially irresponsible in lending support to a growing body of hysterical moralists who were now using the question of drugs as a political and social football.

When this letter appeared in the paper, an Aberdeen mother telephoned me to say that we were not over-estimating the problem; we were under-estimating it. It was a fact that drugs were taken by schoolchildren in Aberdeen. How did she know that? 'My daughter took drugs when a school pupil', she said. The police had no evidence of drug-taking by school-children or of the trafficking of drugs in Aberdeen schools, but during our investigation we had heard a number of reports of drug-taking by city school pupils.

A psychiatric nurse who dealt with drug addicts wrote to say that if our series made even one parent look more carefully and more closely at the life of only one child it could do nothing but good. Another letter dismissed the 'Fair Play' protest as 'utter rubbish'. In the final article in the series we called for more education on the dangers of drugs. 'We must be prepared – all of us – to tackle the problem', we said. No one could have foreseen then that in 1998 Grampian would have the highest proportion of young drug addicts in Scotland.

'Glance back across the centuries', Provost James Rust had said. It reminded me of another quote about turning back the pages of history. It came from Henrik Ibsen's *Ghosts*. 'I've only to pick up a newspaper and I seem to see ghosts gliding between the lines', wrote the playwright. If there were ghosts to be seen in the faded pages of the old *Evening Express* they would have been the ghosts of the men who produced the first ha'penny paper in 1879, and, in particular, William Gillies, its first editor. He was asssistant editor *and* general manager on the *Journal*, edited by William Forsyth, when it was decided to launch a new evening paper. It was Gillies's idea and he was offered the editorship.

The first ha'penny evening paper ran to only four pages, but the readers liked it. There was such a demand for the first edition that the printing machines couldn't cope with it. William Gillies introduced a formula that was still being followed successfully more than a century later – a good mix of local and national news. In its early years it carried such varied stories as a big trial of bank directors in Glasgow, vice in the east end of Aberdeen ('Mothers can't be too careful', warned a baillie), the opening of Union Terrace gardens in 1879, the defeat of the British at Rourke's Drift in the Zulu war ('Terrible scenes of bloodshed' said the heading), the birth of a son to the Countess of Aberdeen (bells were rung and flags raised at Methlick Post Office), and a triumph for a man whose name was to become known wherever roses bloomed. In September, 1879, Messrs James Cocker and Sons won first prize at an international flower show.

Gillies was persuaded to return to the *Journal's* editorial chair in 1890. He had taken over the ha'penny evening paper in a year that had seen the appalling tragedy of the collapse of the Tay Bridge; he left it when another famous bridge – the Forth Road Bridge – was being opened. The date was 4 March, 1890. He had nursed the new paper through an eventful decade. Among other major stories that found their way into the paper were the killing of General Gordon at Khartoum, Queen Victoria celebrating her Jubilee, a new public library planned for Aberdeen, and a Jack the Ripper scare spreading throgh the town when a girl named Helen Watt was savagely attacked in Garvock Wynd.

In March, 1883, four years before Queen Victoria's Jubilee, the *Evening Express* reported the death of her famous servant, John Brown. It made 'quite a sensation in London', according to the 'E.E.', for nobody there knew he was ill. He was said to be 'omnipotent' in the Royal household – 'a distinguished lady was heard to describe him as 'a great rough savage''. The death of another well-known North-east character in the eighties created a bigger stir than the passing of John Brown. He was Duncan Campbell McKinley (better known as Blin' Bob), a blind hawker, singer and writer of broadsheets (see Chapter Four).

Blin' Bob's funeral was described by the *Express* as 'an event that atracted a great amount of public notice'. The Guestrow, Broad Street, Netherkirkgate and St Catherine's Wynd, were lined by thousands of spectators'. There was a curious footnote to the report of his funeral:

We understand that a short time previous to the funeral Mr Max Gregor, Marischal Street, took a plaster cast of McKinlay's head, which was found to be 23½ ins. in circumference, or exactly an inch more than the average cranium.

Mr Gregor explained that this showed that Duncan phrenologically was more than an ordinary character. Had he been possessed of eyesight and education there was no doubt but he would have been a man holding a good position in place of being a wanderer on the streets.

In between reporting the great events of the day, the *Evening Express* kept its readers informed about such weighty events as an outbreak of 'the insidious malady popularly known as 'pink eye' among the city's horse population. Twenty horses owned by the Aberdeen Tramway Company went on the sick list and 'seriously crippled the resources of the company'. The paper also dropped into its pages snippets of news that were often more interesting than the major stories. For instance:

> July 16, 1883
> The death of Tom Thumb is
> announced from New York today.

There was also a 'brief' in 1899 about comic papers in Vienna carrying cartoons which 'coarsely ridiculed' Queen Victoria and the British Army:

The *Daily Telegraph* Paris correspondent states that *Le Rire* is publishing this week another shameful coloured caricature of the Queen and the German Emperor.

During my editorship, Aberdeen and the North-east were stunned by what became known as 'the crime that shocked Scotland' – the murder of a young Mearns farmer, Maxwell Garvie, by his wife Sheila and her lover Brian Tevendale. In *The Granite City* I told how *Evening Express* sales rocketed to record totals during the Garvie trial. But it wasn't the first time this sort of thing had happened. On 12 January, 1899, the paper carried a short story with the headline 'The phenomenal sale of the *Express*'.

This was brought about by a trial at the High Court in Aberdeen of James Robertson, who was charged with the murder of Margaret Wilson in a house in George Street. It was said to have been an exceptionally brutal murder. Medical evidence at the trial unfolded a gory picture of an almost animal-like attack on the victim. 'Gruesome details' said one heading, and the *Evening Express* published them with the sort of relish shown by the sensational tabloids of today.

'Body had evidently been washed after death', said the medical report, 'but parts around private organs still smeared with hardened blood, and soles of both feet more or less covered with a mixture of dried blood and dirt. Two bruised marks, about two inches apart on front of upper part of neck, as if from clutching the throat firmly with the fingers'. The *Evening Express* finally drew the line on the evidence. 'Further details of a shocking description are here given', it said, 'but cannot be published'. James Robertson was found guilty of culpable homicide and sentenced to life imprisonment.

Alongside the verdict was a short piece which told how hansom cabs were sent dashing about Aberdeen and the North-east delivering papers to newsagents desperate for supplies. 'During the early part of yesterday hundreds of telegrams were received from newsagents and others throughout the country ordering additional supplies. The resources of the publishing department were taxed to the utmost, and in the despatch of supplies the carts and customary means of distribution had to be supplemented by the employment of seven hansoms, which were kept busy plying during the afternoon.

'As an indication of the sale by the "man in the street", it may be mentioned that several of the news vendors took supplies of from 20 to 30 dozens'. Not even Aberdeen's legendary newsvendor Patsy Gallagher could have matched that!

So the *Evening Express* surged to success in the last year of the nineteenth century. It augered well for the century to come. When the paper celebrated its 25th anniversary it paused to take stock of its progress. Above a picture showing the start of work on Aberdeen's new Regent Bridge – 'the revolutionary new bridge', said the caption – was the heading: 'Success that spans 25 years'. Below it was a report about changes in the 'E.E.':

It was launched at a time when the halfpenny evening paper was in the experimental stage all over the country and grave and persistent were the predictions that Aberdeen was too small a city for such a venture. That very serious obstacles stood in the way of success cannot be denied. The very facilities for rapid production and printing – the first essentials for an evening paper – were far behind what they are today, and as for advertisers, their faith in the evening paper as an advertising medium was long in coming. These were not slight difficulties, but they were gradually and steadily overcome.

The presses rolled on through the years, the headlines getting bigger as the years passed . . . Kennedy's assassination . . . the Profumo scandal . . . Beatlemania . . . Aberdeen's typhoid outbreak . . . the first man on the

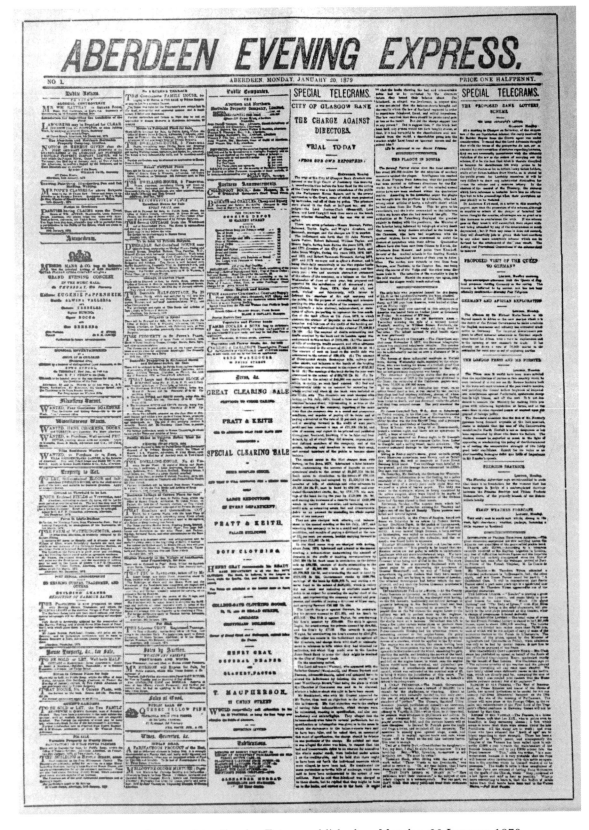

A copy of the *Evening Express* published on Monday, 20 January, 1879.

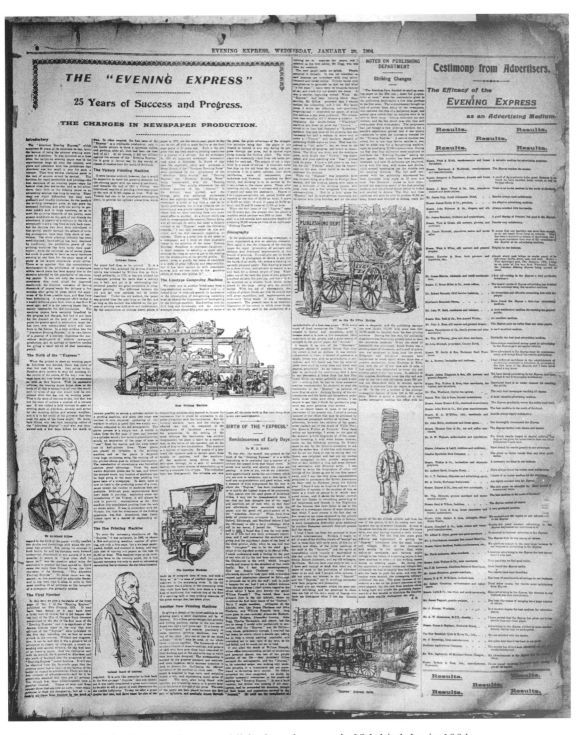

A page from the *Evening Express* published on the paper's 25th birthday in 1904.

Toasting George Fraser's 90th birthday at a lunch held in his honour at the Aberdeen Journals office. Back row, left to right: Harry Roulston, who succeeded Bob Smith as Editor of the *Evening Express*, Ian Hardie, photographer, David Christie, Assistant Editor of the *Evening Express*, Bob Smith, Editor of the *Evening Express*, Peter Watson, Editor of the *Press and Journal*, Jimmy Lees, *Evening Express* news editor. Front, left to right: Dr Cuthbert Graham, George Fraser, Jimmy Grant, Editor of the *Press and Journal*.

Moon . . . Nixon's downfall . . . the Queen pressing the button that set North Sea oil flowing. There were many more, pacing out the final years of my editorship, and on Friday, 25 November, 1983, I at last got a headline to myself – 'E.E. man at the top retires', it said. Scotland's longest daily newspaper editor was retiring early in 1984.

The boy who had licked stamps in McKilliam's old sweetie shop had come to the end of the paper chase. I retired early, but I had few regrets. I had always regarded myself as a 'hands-on' editor, happiest when I was working on the paper, turning out late editions for the big story, planning lay-outs, writing comment pieces, but in the last years I became bogged down in administration, endless boardroom meetings, and arguments with the journalists' union. I had been a member of the NUJ (National Union of Journalists) all my working life, but I became tired and disillusioned by the trouble-making of a handful of extremists. On one occasion I produced the paper myself, single-handed, while the pickets lined up outside. I felt the paper had to come out. After I retired, another strike ended in the dismissal of many good journalists who had been with me for years.

In July, 1998, fourteen years after my retirement, a small group of people gathered in a house in Aberdeen's King's Gate. George Fraser, who was editor of the *Evening Express* from 1944 to 1953, had lived there. He was still writing a weekly column for the *Press and Journal* when he celebrated his 100th birthday. Some time after his death his son George brought together a few of his father's former colleagues and friends at his King's Gate home.

There were familiar faces in that small gathering, among them Jimmy Lees, who came from Stonehaven and was my former news editor; Jack Nicoll, who had been a feature writer and columnist on the paper; Jack Webster, a Maud loon, who left the *Evening Express* to make a name for himself on the *Herald* in Glasgow; Jack Cryle, a photographer with a fine taste for a good whisky; Arthur Binnie, my chief sub-editor for a time; Gordon Forbes, whose brother Jimmy had been my sports writer, and Ethel Simpson, with whom I had shared many a pint in the City Bar when we were reporters together. Ken Peters, himself a former 'E.E.' editor, was also there with his wife Arunda.

We chatted, joked, struggled to remember half-forgotten names and events, put our tongues in our cheeks and told each other how young we still looked, and talked about George and his time with both the *Evening Express* and *Press and Journal.* George spent most of his journalistic life in Broad Street. He held the posts of chief sub-editor of the *Daily Journal* (later the *Press and Journal*) and of the *Evening Express,* and eventually became editor of the evening paper.

They didn't have five-day weeks and eight-hour days when George started his career as a journalist. When I was an office boy there was a sub-editor on the paper called John Ogilvie. On one occasion he told the editor that he would be delayed a little at lunchtime. He came back to the office later than he intended and was profuse in his apologies. He explained that the reason for his delay was that during his lunch-hour he had been getting married.

George was a placid, thoughtful man. He had a quiet humour that was shown in witty verses he penned for the evening paper – and for his own amusement. I often wish I had kept some of them. I remember seeing a poem he wrote about his work as a sub-editor. It was called 'The Subs Lament' and it began 'I'm weary, weary subbin' in this caul' ungodly room . . .' There was a passing reference in it to George Leys Smith, a journalist who was over-fond of food, but who eventually ate his way up to the *Press and Journal* editor's chair. This is what George Fraser wrote about 'Smithy' and the 'subs':

I've hin my share o' murders an' sic like
   bluidy splores,
I've even tried my han' at WRIs,
I've handled spicy stories, retailed them
   tee in scores,
An' found the missin' words in Smithy's
   pies,
I've written heaps o' captions on the
   deeds o' fellow-man,
'I've telt the truth – on paper – aboot
   the quines',
But noo ma broo is wrinkled, ye can
   see my tremblin' hand,
I've wrestled sair – an' canna get my
   lines!'

George climbed out of the sub-editors' caul', ungodly room to take the top editorial post on the *Evening Express*. He was still 'getting his lines' when he chalked up his century. After his death, the gathering of journalists organised by his son was, I think, intended as a kind of last farewell to this Grand Old Man of journalism. But for me it was something more than that. It seemed to me to be the closing of a chapter in my own life. From then on, every time I picked up a newspaper I would see ghosts gliding between the lines.

Postscript

When the 'Scotland the What?' team were playing to full houses, I wanted to run a regular feature from them in the *Evening Express*. Buff Hardie and Steve Robertson came up with a typical Aberdeen couple, 'Dod 'n' Bunty'. Their conversations were written in 'Scotland the What?' style and the weekly feature was soon a firm favourite with readers. Its opening line, 'Far's the paper?' became a catch phrase. It still appears in the 'E.E.' today, the longest running feature in the paper. When I retired in 1984, Dod and Bunty had something to say about it:

Far's the paper?

Ye're nae gettin' it.

Fit wye? There's nae a strike, is there? That wis terrible on Sunday nae gettin' the *News o' the World*. Fit wye are folk expected tae keep up wi' current affairs?

No, no. There is a paper, but ye hinna time tae read it. Ye've tae tak' me up tae Foresterhill.

Yer disc hisna slipped again, has it? Ken 'is, Bunty, ye'll hae tae gi'e up yer karate on a Monday nicht.

No, no. I'm gain' tae the maternity hospital.

FIT? Ye're nae expectin' sextuplets, are ye? It wis bad enough fan ye brocht Tiddles hame tae stop Jimmy Allan fae droonin' her.

No, no. I'm jist gain' tae visit. Here's the paper. Look at the birth announcements.

Far are they? 'Births.' Here we are. 'Edwards. Colin and Alison are still on Cloud Nine following the safe arrival of Karen Louise, a darling step-sister for Justin.' An' fa dis Justin belong til? That's fit I wid like tae ken. Fit kind o' Hippie set-up's that for a bairn tae be brocht up in?

No. Nae that een. The next een. It's Kathleen.

Kathleen fa'?

Kathleen Forbes. Ye mind. Lorraine wis her bridesmaid in February.

February? Far's my home calculator? Cuttin' it pretty fine, isn' she? Fit dis it say aboot her. 'Forbes. To Kathleen and Brian, nee Walker'. That's wrang. It's nae Brian that's nee Walker, its Kathleen that's nee Walker.

That's richt. Brian's nae nee Walker. Brian's nae nee naething.

Hae, wait a minute. Kathleen's nae nee Walker neither. Her name wis Wallace. That's a misprint. That's shockin', that. Ye can easy see Bob Smith's gettin' demob-happy. I've seen the day he would have spotted that.

Fa?

Bob Smith.

Is he an obstetrician?. Would it have been him that pit it in the paper?

No, no, Bunty. The *Evening Express* may deliver the goods, but Bob Smith is not an obstetrician. He's the editor.

Oh, that Bob Smith. My Auntie Alice kent him. She wis his landlady fan he wis a young reporter.

Well, he's been editor for twenty-two years, but he's leavin' now.

Auntie Alice winna be surprised. Fan he got the editor's job she said he wid never settle in it.

Index